MW00814042

Pahrump

A Valley Waiting to Become a City

Pahrump

A Valley Waiting to Become a City

Robert D. McCracken

Nye County Press

TONOPAH NEVADA

All rights reserved. No part of this publication may be reproduced or transmitted in any form or by any means, electronic or mechanical, including photocopy, recording, or any information storage and retrieval system, without permission in writing from the publisher.

PAHRUMP
A Valley Waiting to Become a City
by Robert D. McCracken

Second printing 1992
© Copyright 1990 by Nye County Press

Published in 1990 by Nye County Press
P.O. Box 3070
Tonopah, Nevada 89049

Library of Congress Catalog Card Number: 90-060554
ISBN: 1-878138-53-7

DESIGNED BY PAUL CIRAC, WHITE SAGE STUDIOS, VIRGINIA CITY, NEVADA

PRINTED IN THE UNITED STATES OF AMERICA

To my mother, Martha, and to all
the women who made homes for
their families on the Nevada desert

In appreciation for their unwavering support and encouragement for the Nye County Town History Project:

Nye County Commissioners

Robert "Bobby" N. Revert
Joe S. Garcia, Jr.
Richard L. Carver
Barbara J. Raper

and Nye County Planning Consultant

Stephen T. Bradhurst, Jr.

Contents

Preface

Historians generally consider the year 1890 as the close of the American frontier. By then, most of the western United States had been settled, ranches and farms developed, communities established, and roads and railroads constructed. The mining boomtowns, based on the lure of overnight riches from newly developed lodes, were but a memory.

Although Nevada was granted statehood in 1864, examination of any map of the state from the late 1800s shows that although much of the state was mapped and its geographical features named, a vast region — stretching from Belmont south to the Las Vegas meadows, comprising most of Nye County— remained largely unsettled and unmapped. In 1890 most of southcentral Nevada remained very much a frontier, and it continued to be so for at least another twenty years. Even Las Vegas, now a major urban center, did not get its start as a city until 1905, quite late in comparison to the vast majority of cities in the American West.

The great mining booms at Tonopah (1900), Goldfield (1902), and Rhyolite (1904) represent the last major flowering of what might be called the Old West. Consequently, southcentral Nevada, notably Nye County—perhaps more than any other region of the West—remains close to the American frontier. In a real sense, a significant part of the frontier can still be found there. It exists in the attitudes, values, lifestyles, and memories of area residents. The frontier-like character of the area also is visible in the relatively undisturbed condition of the natural environment, most of it essentially untouched by humans.

Aware of Nye County's close ties to our nation's frontier past and the scarcity of written sources on local history (especially after 1920), the Nye County Board of Commissioners initiated the Nye County Town History Project (NCTHP) in 1987. The NCTHP is an effort to systematically collect and preserve the history of Nye County. The centerpiece of the NCTHP is a large set of interviews conducted with individuals who had knowledge of local history. The interviews provide a composite view of community and county history, revealing the flow of life and events for a part of Nevada that has heretofore been largely neglected by historians. Each interview was recorded, transcribed, and then edited lightly to preserve the language and speech patterns of those interviews. All oral history interviews have been printed on acid-free paper and bound and archived in Nye County libraries, Special Collections in the James R. Dickinson Library at the University of Nevada, Las Vegas, and at other archival sites located throughout Nevada.

Collection of the oral histories has been accompanied by the assembling of a set of photographs depicting each community's history. These pictures have been obtained from participants in the oral history interviews and other present and past Nye County residents. Complete sets of these photographs have been archived along with the oral histories.

The oral histories and photo collections, as well as written sources, served as the basis for the preparation of this volume on Pahrump history. It is one in a series of volumes on the history of all major Nye County communities.

In a real sense this volume, like the others in the NCTHP series, is the result of a community effort. Before the oral interviews were conducted, a number of local residents provided advice on which community members had lived in the area the longest, possessed and recalled information not available to others, and were available and willing to participate. Because of time and budgetary constraints, many highly qualified persons were not interviewed.

Following the interviews, the participants gave even more of their time and energy: They elaborated upon and clarified points made during the taped interviews; they went through family albums and identified photographs; and they located books, dates, family records, and so forth. During the preparation of this manuscript, a number of community members were contacted, sometimes repeatedly (if asked, some would probably readily admit that they felt pestered), to answer questions that arose during the writing and editing of the manuscript. Moreover, once the manuscript was in more or less final form, each individual who was discussed for more than a paragraph or two in the text was provided with a copy of his or her portion of the text and was asked to check that portion for errors. Appropriate changes were then made in the manuscript.

Once that stage was completed, several individuals in Pahrump were asked to review the entire manuscript for errors of omission and commission. At each stage, this quality-control process resulted in the elimination of factual errors and raised our confidence in the validity of the contents.

The author's training as an anthropologist, not a historian (although the difference between the disciplines is probably less than some might suppose), likely has something to do with the community approach taken in the preparation of this volume. It also may contribute to the focus on the details of individuals and their families as opposed to a general description of local residents and their communities. Perhaps this volume, as well as a concern with variability among individuals and their contribution to a community, reflects an "ethnographic," as opposed to a "historical," perspective on local history. In the author's view, there is no such thing as "the history" of a community; there are many histories of a community. A community's history is like a sunrise — the colors are determined by a multitude of factors, such as the time of year, weather, and point of view. This history of Pahrump was greatly determined by the input of those who helped produce it. If others had participated, both the subjects treated and the relative emphasis the subjects received would have been, at least, somewhat different. Many basic facts would, of course, remain much the same—such things as names, dates, and locations of events. But the focus, the details illustrating how facts and human beings come together, would have been different. History is, and always will remain, sensitive to perspective and impressionistic, in the finest and most beautiful sense of the word.

A longer and more thoroughly referenced (though non-illustrated) companion to this volume, titled *A History of Pahrump, Nevada,* is also available through Nye County Press. Virtually all written material contained in the present volume was obtained from the longer volume. Those who desire more comprehensive referencing should consult the longer version of Pahrump history.

I hope readers enjoy this illustrated history of Pahrump, Nevada. Pahrump is an interesting and scenic place, brimming with a frontier community's enthusiasm for the future. A beautiful desert valley with vast land and water resources, clean air, and plenty of sunshine, it stands on the threshold of its destiny: to become a lovely city.

Robert D. McCracken

Acknowledgments

This volume was produced under the Nye County Town History Project, initiated by the Nye County Board of Commissioners. Appreciation goes to Chairman Joe S. Garcia, Jr., Robert "Bobby" N. Revert, and Pat Mankins; Mr. Revert and Mr. Garcia, in particular, showed deep interest and unyielding support for the project from its inception. Thanks also go to current commissioners Richard L. Carver and Barbara J. Raper, who have since joined Mr. Revert on the board and who have continued the project with enthusiastic support. Stephen T. Bradhurst, Jr., planning consultant for Nye County, gave unwavering support and advocacy, provided advice and input regarding the conduct of the research, and constantly served as a sounding board as production problems were worked out. This volume would never have been possible without the enthusiastic support of the Nye County commissioners and Mr. Bradhurst.

Thanks go to the participants of the Nye County Town History Project, especially those from Pahrump, who kindly provided much of the information; thanks, also, to residents from Pahrump and throughout southern Nevada — too numerous to mention by name — who provided assistance, historical information, and photographs, many of which are included in this volume.

Jean Charney and Jean Stoess did the word processing and, along with Gary Roberts, Maire Hayes, and Jodie Hanson, provided editorial comments, review, and suggestions. Alice Levine and Michelle Starika edited several drafts of the manuscript and contributed measurably to this volume's scholarship and readability; Alice Levine also served as production consultant. Gretchen Loeffler and Bambi McCracken assisted in numerous secretarial and clerical duties. Gordon Loeffler and Donn Knepp copied photographs; Paul Cirac, who was raised in central Nevada, was responsible for the design and layout of this book.

Harry Ford, M. Kent "Tim" Hafen, Jackie Hafen, Deke Lowe, and Celesta Lowe, who know more about Pahrump history than anybody, kindly critiqued several drafts of the manuscript. Their assistance and support have been invaluable, and although I pestered them with many questions, they never gave evidence of impatience. Roland Wiley also critiqued a draft of the manuscript, and Jacque Ruud and Leon Hughes provided clarification of facts. Noella Benvenuti, registrar, San Bernardino County Museums, Redlands, California, provided access to the museum's data file on the Yount family and graciously provided copies of a number of photographs reproduced in this volume. Kevin Rafferty and Lynda Blair, from the University of Nevada, Las Vegas, Environmental Research Center, provided helpful suggestions on the section concerning the archaeology of Native Americans in the Pahrump–Las Vegas area. Phillip Earl of the Nevada Historical Society contributed valuable support and criticism throughout, and Tom King at the Oral History Program of the University of Nevada, Reno, served as consulting oral historian. Susan Jarvis of Special Collections, James R. Dickinson Library, University of Nevada, Las Vegas, assisted greatly with research conducted at that institution. Much deserved thanks are extended to all these persons.

All aspects of production of this volume were supported by the U.S. Department of Energy, Grant No. DE-FG08-89NV10820. However, any opinions, findings, conclusions, or recommendations expressed herein are those of the author and do not necessarily reflect the views of DOE. Any errors and deficiencies are, of course, the author's responsibility.

R. D. M.

Pahrump

A Valley Waiting to Become a City

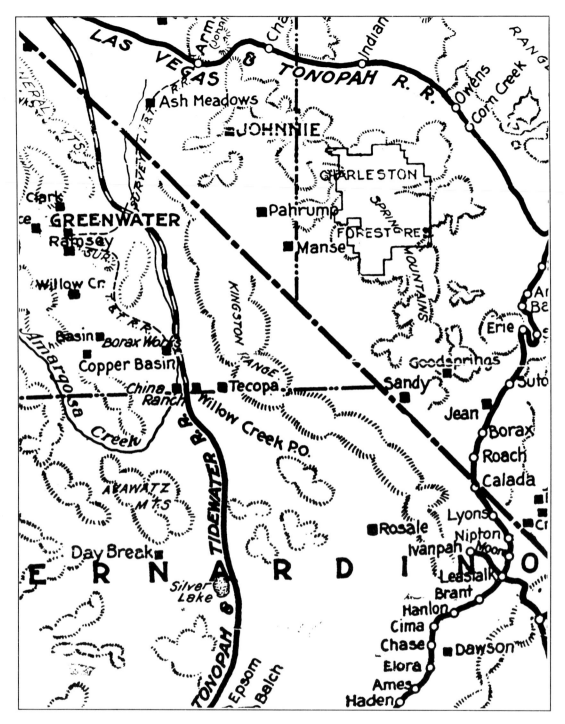

Portion of map of the state of Nevada, published by the Clason Map Co., Denver, Colorado, in 1906, showing the Pahrump Valley and neighboring communities. Note the Pahrump and Manse ranches are shown as separate communities.

Central Nevada Museum

CHAPTER ONE

Early History of the Pahrump Valley

T he availability of water has always determined the possibilities of life in the arid
American West. For untold thousands of years, the magnificent springs located in
the Pahrump Valley of Nevada have formed the basis of a community consisting of numerous
plant and animal species. For what might be as much as 12,000 years, the springs have served
to sustain a variety of cultures and ways of life, and in recent years they have made possible
the beginnings of the growth of a modern city. This volume attempts to briefly tell the story of
the many different groups and individuals who have lived in the Pahrump Valley and the ways
in which they have used its water and land.

The Physical Setting

The Pahrump Valley is located in Nye and Clark counties, Nevada, and Inyo and San
Bernardino counties, California, and extends over approximately 1050 square miles. The valley
is bounded on the north and east by the great Spring Mountains massif; Mount Sterling,
elevation 8217 feet, lies to the north and Charleston Peak, elevation 11,918 feet, to the east. The
Pahrump Valley lies in the same relationship to the west side of the Spring Mountains as does
the Las Vegas Valley to the east side.

Much of the valley floor is between 2500 and 2800 feet above sea level, making a maximum
topographic relief of more than 9000 feet between the valley floor and the mountaintop. The
Pahrump Valley is a ground-water basin underlain and enclosed on all sides by impermeable
bedrock.

Water has been the focal point of the history of the Pahrump Valley since its first occupation
by human beings. Large, free-flowing springs were present on the lower aprons of the
Pahrump and Manse alluvial fans when Europeans first arrived. Water in the valley's aquifer

1

comes entirely from precipitation; nearly all is from moisture deposited on the west slope of the Spring Mountains. Average annual precipitation in southern Nevada is between 4 and 8 inches, yet 8 to 16 inches fall in the Spring Mountains, with even more precipitation at higher elevations.

It is estimated that between 1916 and 1937 approximately 9600 acre-feet of water were discharged from the aquifer per year, most of it from springs. Over 7000 acre-feet of this discharge took place in the vicinity of the Pahrump Ranch and most of the remainder in the Manse Ranch area. The annual ground-water increment to Pahrump Valley is approximately 23,000 acre-feet.

The Pahrump Valley is several degrees cooler than the Las Vegas Valley (which in turn is cooler than the Moapa Valley). Maximum temperatures in Pahrump are about the same as in Las Vegas, but lower minimums in all months result in a greater range of temperatures, later springs, earlier fall frosts, and shorter growing seasons. Light frosts usually occur in the valley between the months of November and March.

Origin of the Word "Pahrump"

In 1872, George M. Wheeler described the "Pah-rimp Desert and the Pah-rimp Springs," at which resided "quite a number of Pah-ute Indians." A number of meanings for the word Pahrump have been suggested, including "water-stone" from the Southern Paiute, *pah*, meaning "water," and *timpi*, meaning "stone," modified phonetically to *rimpi* or *rumpi*; Parumpaiats, a Southern Paiute Indian band from in or near the Moapa Valley; or "Great Spring," "water-mouth," "big flow of water," "big orifice," or "cave from which water flows," from Southern Paiute (Carlson, 1974:185). Local Native American residents in the Pahrump Valley have suggested that the word has no meaning—that it is a name whose only reference for the local Paiute Indians was the Pahrump Spring.

The First Human Occupants of the Pahrump Valley

The first human beings to occupy the Pahrump-Las Vegas area were members of the Tule Springs culture, named for the archaeological site at Tule Springs, located just north of Las Vegas on the east side of the Spring Mountains. The Tule Springs phase, which lasted from about 13,000 to 10,000 years ago, is usually considered the Paleo-Indian, or Big Game Hunter, phase of Nevada prehistory. These early inhabitants produced the well-known Clovis point, one of which has been found on the west side of the Las Vegas Valley. They are thought to have subsisted on the mammoths, camels, horses, and other big game that probably roamed on the shores of the lake that existed at the site of the present dry lake bed in Pahrump Valley. Additionally, they probably gathered many plants and hunted small game. They are thought to have occupied large base camps in the lowlands, where band-sized groups lived.

About 7500 years ago the climate became noticeably drier and warmer, leading to the Desert Culture phase of human occupation. Lakes on the valley floors probably dried up and many large game species vanished or became extinct. Inhabitants were probably nomadic, exploiting foods from the valley floors to mountain tops.

Around 5000 years ago, the climate in southern Nevada and the Great Basin began to cool, and there was somewhat greater precipitation. Archaeological sites from this phase are found at a variety of elevations and physiographic features in southern Nevada, including valley springs, mountain foothills, desert zones, well-watered canyons, and higher elevation juniper-piñon pine zones. Many rock shelters in southern Nevada were occupied. Some recent research indicates that the Native American occupants of the Pahrump Valley in this era, as well as their neighbors in the Las Vegas Valley and the Moapa area, were the ancestors of the Southern

Paiute, who occupied much of southern Nevada at the time of the first white contact and whose descendants remain in the Pahrump Valley and Las Vegas area today.

The next era in the archaeological history of the Pahrump Valley, the Virgin Anasazi phase, began about 2000 years ago and lasted until about A.D. 1200. The Anasazi are the ancestors of the modern Pueblo Indians, including the Hopi of Arizona, the Zuni in western New Mexico, and Pueblo Indians who live along the Rio Grande in northern New Mexico. The Anasazi moved into southern Nevada around the time of the birth of Christ and occupied areas along the Colorado River and in the regions of the Virgin and Muddy rivers.

The Anasazi entry into extreme southern Nevada is believed to have been associated with the mining of salt and the extraction of turquoise from mines located not far from the present location of Hoover Dam near Crescent Pass and the Halloran Springs area. For this span of 1200 years, artifacts from the Anasazi and the original occupants of the Pahrump Valley-Las Vegas area are found in close association. Some experts believe that the intrusion of the Anasazi did not threaten the peoples living in the region—presumably ancestors of modern Southern Paiute—and that, in fact, the Paiute and Anasazi developed a symbiotic relationship in which the Paiutes may have worked for the Anasazi as laborers (Rafferty and Blair, 1984:62-63). The coming of the Anasazi may well have been seen as an advantage by the Paiute, representing a new source of mates and trade and an information exchange.

Approximately 800 years ago, the Anasazi abandoned the Pahrump-Las Vegas area. Researchers disagree about the reasons for this abandonment. There is evidence of a major drought about 800 years ago (A.D. 1150), which might have made agriculture more difficult by reducing the flow of water in the Muddy and Virgin river areas. There may have been overexploitation of wild resources such as agave and other foods. It has also been suggested that there was a collapse in the pan-southwestern trading system. With the collapse of the trading network, there was little reason for the Anasazi to maintain their southern Nevada outpost, especially in the face of reduced resources produced by drought, and thus the area was abandoned.

An alternative hypothesis that some scholars favor suggests that about the time of the abandonment of southern Nevada by the Anasazi, the ancestors of the modern Numic-speakers, the linguistic group to which the Southern Paiute belong, entered the area and, in effect, drove out a group of earlier inhabitants who spoke a language we are unable to identify today (perhaps an extinct language or perhaps a language spoken by some neighboring group). This explanation fits with linguistic evidence indicating that the Numic-speaking peoples, including the Southern Paiute, Shoshone, and Utes, entered the Great Basin from southern California approximately 1000 years ago.

The Southern Paiute Indians

The last stage in the archaeological history of the Native Americans of Pahrump Valley is known as the Paiute phase, which began about 800 years ago. Researchers believe that the present-day Southern Paiute are descended from people who have lived in the southern Nevada region for at least the past 800 years.

The Southern Paiute have often been characterized as "poor" and bearers of a "simple" culture; the fact is that they developed a way of life admirably suited to the land and its resources. The Southern Paiute occupy a portion of southeastern California, southern Nevada, southwestern Utah, and northern Arizona. Their language belongs to the Southern Numic branch of the Uto-Aztecan linguistic family. Within historical times, sixteen identifiable Southern Paiute groups, or bands, existed, residing in the area bounded by Navajo Mountain in southern Utah to Sevier Lake in southwestern Utah to the Amargosa Range, located west of Ash Meadows in California, and to Blythe, California, on the Arizona-California border.

Indian summer camp, Pahrump Valley, Nevada, circa 1900.

University of Nevada at Las Vegas – Dickinson Library Special Collections

Among the Southern Paiute there was no overall tribal organization and each of the sixteen bands had its own territory and was, for the most part, economically self-sufficient. The Southern Paiute were what anthropologists call hunters and gatherers; that is to say, they subsisted by foraging for wild plants and animals, sometimes supplementing their food supply by agriculture. Because the bands occupied a wide variety of environments, they differed somewhat in the foods they exploited.

Southern Paiute occupying the Pahrump Valley have been called, by whites, the Las Vegas band. Their name for themselves is Nipakanticimi, which means "people of Charleston Peak" (Kelly and Fowler, 1986:395).

Like all Southern Paiute, members of the Las Vegas band lived a seminomadic way of life and moved about in their territory as food resources became available. They lived and traveled in small, flexible groups with the family as the basic unit of social organization. Sometimes a single family lived alone in an isolated spot. At other times, several families congregated at a large water source. Camps occupied for any length of time were always associated with springs and sources of flowing water. Plants gathered by the Las Vegas band of Paiute included pine nuts, mesquite beans, screw beans, Indian spinach, agave, berries of several varieties, and many kinds of grass seeds. They hunted animals such as rabbits, small rodents, desert tortoises, big horn sheep, deer, and many varieties of birds, including quail. The Las Vegas Paiute used poison arrows. The poison was produced by having a rattlesnake bite a piece of deer's liver,

Chief Tecopa (center), circa 1900. The men with him are thought to be Harsha White (left) and Joseph Yount.

University of Nevada at Las Vegas – Dickinson Library Special Collections

Chief Tecopa

The most famous Southern Paiute "chief" was Tecopa, who was probably born about 1815 in the Las Vegas area and died in Pahrump in 1904. He was a leader for the Ash Meadows and Pahrump region. Tecopa's life spanned a period of tumultuous change for the Paiute. He is reported to have first seen whites at Indian Springs when some men who called themselves "mountain men" stopped to rest their horses and secure food for their journey to the west. One is said to have been a mean-looking individual with one leg carved out of a stump of a tree whom the others called "Pegleg Smith," a notorious trapper and horse thief. Tecopa's residence was at the Pahrump Spring, and he was the *pakwinavi* of Southern Paiute villages at Pahrump, Tecopa, Potosi Spring, and Horse Thief Springs in the Kingston Range. A *pakwinavi*, or "big talker," was a kind of regional chief whose official function was to organize rabbit drives and the fall festival—the large communal gathering among surrounding communities following the pine-nut harvest.

Chief Tecopa had a reputation as a peacemaker; for many years, he tried to convince tribal members that killing and stealing were not productive, especially when white men, who had guns and far outnumbered the Indians, were affected. The present community of Tecopa is named after this Paiute leader.

Indian family, Pahrump Valley, Nevada, circa 1900.

University of Nevada at Las Vegas – Dickinson Library Special Collections

which was buried in the ground until it became putrid. It was then removed from the ground and allowed to dry and, when steeped in water, was rubbed on arrows.

The families harvested foods as they ripened. They had detailed and intimate knowledge of their resources and knew where foods would be available at a given time of year. They stored foods, particularly pine nuts, for the winter. Men usually were responsible for hunting, and women tended to focus their activities on the collection of plant foods.

In addition to hunting and gathering, the Southern Paiute practiced agriculture around springs and streams. A small garden might cover an acre, with larger plots jointly maintained by relatives. Sometimes ditch irrigation systems were constructed. Red and white corn were commonly grown by the Southern Paiute but yellow maize was not reported among the Las Vegas group.

The Southern Paiute occupied dwellings made from brush and tree limbs. The Southern Paiute's basic dress was a double apron made of skin or vegetable fiber. Skin capes and rabbitskin robes were worn by both sexes. The chief craft was the manufacture of baskets, which were used for winnowing, parching, and beating of seeds, and as water jugs when coated with piñon pitch. Men tanned hides using the brains and marrow from the spinal cord of the animal as tanning agents. The Las Vegas Paiute produced pottery.

There was no central political control or organization among the Southern Paiute. Most large economic clusters had a head man who acted more as an adviser than an authority.

The Paiute in the Pahrump-Las Vegas area loved to travel, and they made journeys of great distances. Men from the Las Vegas band traveled to the Pacific Coast "just to look around" and to obtain shell. On rare occasions they would journey to the Hopi villages in northern Arizona, several hundred miles away. The Southern Paiute, who always traveled on foot, rejected the horse when it was introduced to the area, believing that the animal was too much trouble to feed and was, furthermore, damaging to the environment.

The Traditional Southern Paiute Way of Life Comes to an End

The Southern Paiute were able to practice their way of life uninfluenced by the lifestyles of the white man until the early nineteenth century. At first, contact with whites was sporadic and traditional Indian ways were largely untouched. But these sporadic contacts were followed by a trickle of explorers entering Paiute lands. The explorers, in turn, were followed by the development of trails across Paiute land and then by the coming of hundreds of miners seeking the riches the land held. The miners provided a market for the ranches that were soon established at every available spring in the area. Within the memory of a single individual, such as Chief Tecopa, the wild game in the mountains was reduced in number and the Southern Paiute were displaced from their ancestral camps and garden sites at watering holes such as Manse and Pahrump springs.

With their traditional sources of subsistence compromised, the Indians were forced to become more dependent upon white civilization. They found themselves ensconced in white culture, working as wage laborers in the mines and on the ranches and lacking the freedom to roam the vast area they had so long called home. By 1905 Harsha White, a member of the family that developed the ranch at the Manse Springs, stated that the Paiute Indian population had decreased by 60 percent since 1890, a decrease he attributed to "the white man's whiskey and biscuits and love" ("Indian Powwow...," 1905).

Early Explorers and Others in the Pahrump Valley Area

No one can name the European who first set eyes on the Pahrump Valley. It might have been an unknown Spanish miner or explorer working out of Mexico sometime prior to 1825. One possible candidate is Peter Skene Ogden. Historians believe that, in 1826, Ogden was the second white man to set foot in what is now the state of Nevada. In 1829, Ogden again entered the state from the north, traveling from the Carson Sink past Walker Lake to the state's southernmost tip. South of Walker Lake, Ogden and his party are said to have traveled parallel to the present Nevada-California border, eventually reaching the Gulf of California before returning to Oregon. In doing so, it is conceivable that they viewed the Pahrump Valley.

In his expeditions to southern California in 1826 and 1827, Jedediah Smith followed the Colorado River along Nevada's southernmost border, but there is nothing to suggest that he ever left the river far enough to find the Pahrump Valley. Jedediah Smith, however, is credited with linking the two arms of a previously unconnected trail between Santa Fe, New Mexico, and California. The eastern part of the trail was originally explored by the Dominguez-Escalante Expedition and the western by Father Francisco Garces. The combined trail became known as the Old Spanish Trail. Four years after the two arms of the trail were linked, the first pack mule trains began making the passage from Santa Fe to southern California.

Meanwhile, alternative routes that eliminated the Colorado River portion of the trail were being explored. In 1829, Antonio Armijo, a New Mexico merchant, traveled down the Nevada side of the Colorado River and camped at the Las Vegas Wash. In the meantime, a member of the party, a little-known man named Rafael Rivera, had gone looking for a shortcut that had a water supply. Rivera returned and the party entered the Las Vegas Valley, but opinions differ concerning the shortcut taken. The traditional view is that the party went to Cottonwood

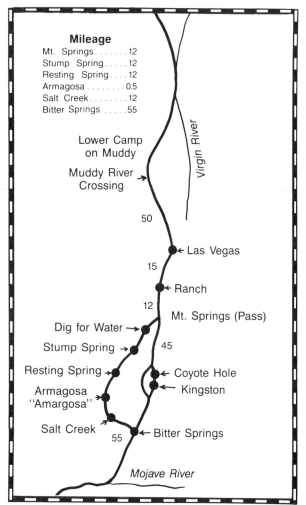

Mileage

Mt. Springs	12
Stump Spring	12
Resting Spring	12
Armagosa	0.5
Salt Creek	12
Bitter Springs	55

Silas Cox, a cowboy and freighter, made sixteen trips between Salt Lake City and San Bernardino from 1862 to 1868. In 1924, he drew a map from memory of the route from the Virgin River in southern Nevada to the Mojave River in southern California. The map shows the distances that Cox remembered between available water on the Nevada portion of the Mormon Trail. Cox's recollection may not have been completely accurate; the presence of water between Mountain Springs and Stump Spring has been questioned. (Map by R. Gary Raham, after original in Reeder, 1966)

Springs and then over the Spring Mountains and into the Pahrump Valley. A more recent interpretation is that the party headed south across Jean Dry Lake and camped at Goodsprings Valley (Warren, 1974). A later route left the Virgin River near Bunkerville, Nevada, and crossed the Mormon Mesa to the Muddy River. From there it was a 55- to 60-mile journey to Las Vegas. This later became part of the route from Salt Lake to California, known as the Mormon Trail. Although a number of alternate shortcuts across southern Nevada were found, all were limited by the availability of water until the Mojave River was reached.

Alternate routes out of Las Vegas usually began west of Las Vegas at Mountain Springs and converged at Bitter Springs about 30 miles from the junction of the trail with the Mojave River. The traditional route of the Old Spanish Trail across the Pahrump Valley involved a stop at Stump Spring and another at Resting Spring, also known as Archilleta and as Agua de Hernandez (named by Fremont for the head of the party massacred there by Indians, whose two survivors he encountered in 1844). From Resting Spring the route went to Amargosa and Salt Creek and on to Bitter Springs. In 1851, Resting Spring was described as having "good feed and water," and travelers were advised to "lay by and rest your animals for the desert" (Reeder, 1966:396). The first wagon route followed the above route, but soon a shortcut developed which bore to the left from Mountain Springs and ran directly to Kingston Spring and then to Bitter Springs.

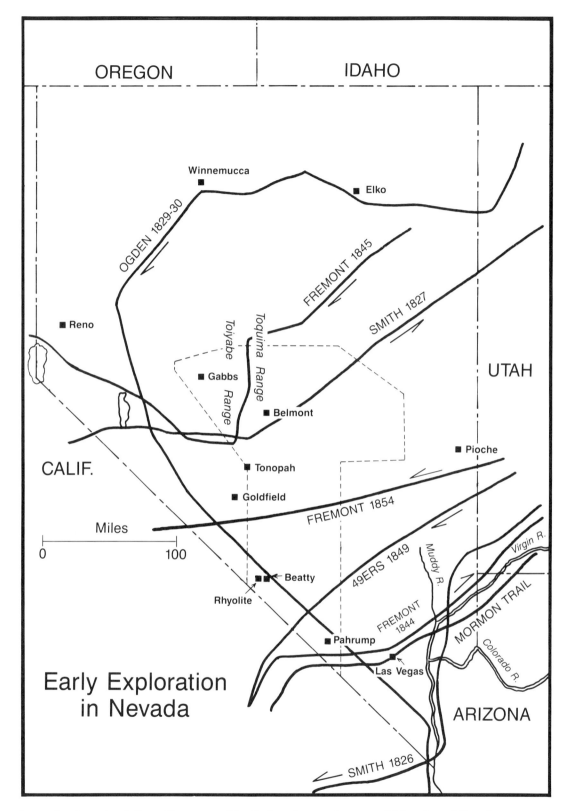

OREGON IDAHO

■ Winnemucca ■ Elko

OGDEN 1829-30

FREMONT 1845

SMITH 1827

■ Reno

Toiyabe Range

Toquima Range

UTAH

■ Gabbs

■ Belmont

■ Pioche

CALIF.

■ Tonopah

■ Goldfield

Miles

0 100

FREMONT 1854

49ERS 1849

Virgin R.

Muddy R.

■ Beatty

Rhyolite

FREMONT 1844

MORMON TRAIL

Colorado R.

Early Exploration
in Nevada

■ Pahrump

Las Vegas

ARIZONA

SMITH 1826

Approximate routes followed by some of the first explorers who crossed Nevada and Nye County:
Smith, 1826, 1827; Ogden, 1829–1830; and Fremont, 1844, 1845, 1854. Also shown is the route of the
forty-niners and the Mormon Trail, which was used from 1830 until after 1869.

Map by R. Gary Raham

A group gathered in front of the Manse Ranch, Pahrump Valley, Nevada, around 1900. Most of the individuals are not identified. Maude Yount White is second from the right. Sam Yount, son of Pahrump Valley pioneer Joseph Yount, is fourth from the right.   San Bernardino County Museum – Fisk Collection

CHAPTER TWO

Settlement and Growth

B y the 1870s, the time was ripe for white settlers to begin taking advantage of the water resources in the Pahrump Valley as well as other sites in the area, including the Amargosa and Ash Meadows area, Oasis Valley to the north, and the Las Vegas Valley, where O. D. Gass had settled at the location of the old Mormon Fort some years earlier. The Indians, of course, had long utilized the springs in the Pahrump Valley and the resources that the abundant water nourished.

Mormon Charlie, a progressive Paiute, is credited with starting the first ranch in the Pahrump Valley. He used stock left behind by miners at Potosi and began his ranch at the Manse Springs in the late 1860s. Chief Tecopa had a rancheria at Pahrump Springs by 1875.

In the spring of 1875, Charles Bennett and his family moved in next to Tecopa at Pahrump Springs and established a ranch. Bennett was a man who always seemed willing to try something new. By 1880, he had several hundred acres in crops, with miles of irrigation ditches and fences. He was the first to mechanize in the valley, purchasing a "mammoth, self-binding harvest machine" in the spring of 1880 (Lingenfelter, 1986:169). While owner of the Pahrump Ranch, Bennett thrived, accumulating horses, mules, and cattle; he had money in a Los Angeles bank. Bennett sold his Pahrump Ranch to Aaron and Rosie Winters for $20,000 in 1882, $15,000 in cash and the balance in mortgages.

Aaron Winters has been described as a "chubby little man with a round, ruddy face and a bushy goatee, a middle-aged midwesterner and a former hotel keeper" (Lingenfelter, 1986:174). He and his wife, Rosie, were living on a small ranch in Ash Meadows when a man named Henry Spiller stopped at their place for the night. Spiller showed Winters how to test for borax by pouring sulfuric acid on borax salts, then adding alcohol, and setting the mixture afire. A green flame would indicate that the salts were borax. Winters remembered seeing some salts in Death Valley similar to those Spiller had shown him. After Spiller left, he and Rosie returned to the site he remembered, which was located a few miles north of Furnace Creek in Death Valley. That night they tested their samples and Winters reportedly exclaimed, "She burns green, Rosie! We're rich, by God!" (Lingenfelter, 1986:174). Winters staked out 27 claims on the property and sold them for $20,000 to William T. Coleman, who was heavily involved in the distribution of borax. Borax was used in the chemical industry and as a laundering additive. With that money Winters bought the Pahrump Ranch from Bennett.

Winters' luck did not hold, however. The market for the products grown at the ranch declined. Winters took in partners to try to keep the ranch going, and he also turned to prospecting, but all to no avail. In 1887 back taxes took all but a small part of the ranch. Rosie had died two or three years after they moved to the ranch, and after the turn of the century Winters had lost all his investment and had become "a virtual hermit in the Shadow Mountains" (Lingenfelter, 1986:175).

Joseph Yount Acquires the Manse Ranch

Mormon Charlie's ranch at Manse Springs was taken over by the Jordan brothers in 1876, and they sold it to Joseph Yount and his family early the next year. Joseph Yount was a frontiersman who had served in the Mexican War with General Stephen Kearney. He went to California in 1849 with the gold rush. He returned to Missouri in 1853 and married Margaret, with whom he would spend the rest of his life. In 1856, he was chosen captain of a train of 100 wagons bound for Oregon. In 1876 he and his family were living in La Grande, Oregon, when he heard of the gold strike at Tombstone, Arizona. He decided to go to Tombstone and disposed of his holdings in Oregon and put together an assembly of wagons, horses, and cattle.

In June 1876, Yount headed south accompanied by his wife, Margaret; their eight children ranging in age from 1 to 17 years; C. W. Turner and his wife and two children; and Yount's son-in-law Harsha White, his wife Maude, and their daughter, Della May, who was 1 year old.

Margaret Yount, wife of Joseph Yount, circa 1900.
San Bernadino County Museum – Fisk Collection

White was born in 1850 in Lawrence County, Pennsylvania, and moved to Missouri at an early age. He graduated from the University of Missouri, moved to Oregon when he was 20, and worked as a school teacher. He married Maude B. Yount in 1872.

By October 1876 the group had reached the Pahranagat Valley in Lincoln County, Nevada. Yount and Towner rented pasture there to rest the cattle before continuing the journey.

In the meantime, Yount changed his mind about going to Tombstone and decided to head for southern California. He took several days to scout ahead for a route. The route he selected took him to the Groom Mine, then 60 miles without water to Indian Springs, and then to Ash Meadows, where the cattle could feed and rest. Harsha White and his wife and daughter remained in Hiko, Nevada, during the winter of 1876, where Mrs. White taught school. The Whites joined the Younts at the Manse Ranch the following summer.

Harsha White, co-developer of the Manse
Ranch, Pahrump Valley, Nevada, circa 1900.

San Bernadino County Museum – Fisk Collection

Maude Yount White, daughter of Joseph and
Margaret Yount, wife of Harsha White, circa
1900.

San Bernadino County Museum – Fisk Collection

Daughters of Joseph and Margaret Yount, in the last quarter of the nineteenth century. From left,
Laura, Maude, Joanna, and Nellie Yount.

San Bernadino County Museum – Fisk Collection

At this point, fate intervened for the Younts. While in Ash Meadows, Yount took his horses to the mountains near the future location of the Johnnie Mine. He left them in the hills above the Pahrump Valley and went to the mining camp of Tecopa to obtain supplies for his family. Upon returning, he found, to his horror, that Indians, having identified the draft horses by their collar marks, had killed all of them. The Indians—likely led by the renegade Horseshutem— knew that if they killed the draft horses, the Younts would not be able to move on with their wagons and the Indians would be free to poach on Yount's cattle, which they would butcher and use as a source of dried meat.

Yount returned to the camp in Ash Meadows, where Mrs. Yount and the children had remained. Because they had heard a rumor that a white family was living 30 miles away at the Pahrump Ranch, Yount headed in that direction the next morning. From the mountains he could see a green spot in the valley; it was the Pahrump Ranch. When he arrived at the oasis, he found Charles Bennett with his wife and two children. Yount told Bennett of his troubles and was informed that the Indians who had killed his horses were renegades. Bennett said that the Paiute were peaceful and many worked on his ranch. He had no draft horses to trade, but he informed Yount that he might be able to trade for a ranch 6 miles away owned by three brothers named Jordan. Yount went to the Manse Springs and traded his cattle for the Jordan brothers' place, which was quite undeveloped.

There was a 12x14-foot house, consisting of posts set in the ground with willows nailed to them and mud filled in over the willows, and a sod roof and floor. Yount planted a garden, and by summer he had plenty of produce to sell at the Tecopa Mine, where he could charge almost any price he wished. During the summer of 1877 he made enough to buy food and clothing for the family that winter. High priority was given to the construction of sleeping quarters for the children—mesquite poles against which corn fodder and stalks were leaned for sides. This

Pahrump Valley, Nevada, around 1900.

San Bernadino County Museum – Fisk Collection

Porch and garden on the Manse Ranch, Pahrump Valley, Nevada, around 1900.

San Bernadino County Museum – Fisk Collection

material was also used for the roof. Since no school was available, in the fall of 1878 Yount sent all of his younger children to school in San Bernardino.

Yount, Harsha White, and Yount's oldest son, Sam Yount, took additional land under lease, planting large amounts of barley and corn. They were successful enough to eventually purchase modern machinery, including mowers, headers, and threshers. Since there were Pacific Coast Borax operations at Furnace Creek and the mines in El Dorado Canyon, Yount could sell everything he raised.

Success on the ranch provided time for prospecting in the Spring Mountain area. Yount and Harsha White were instrumental in forming the Yellow Pine Mining District. Chief Tecopa showed Yount the location of the Boss Mine and the Columbia Mine, both having been previously worked by an old-time prospector who thought the dark copper ore was silver.

The prices ranchers such as the Younts received in the 1870s and 1880s for their crops showed a greater per ton value than much of the ore being dug by the men in the mining camps. Alfalfa was worth between $70 and $200 a ton and an acre could yield 6 tons a year. Barley brought $200 a ton and 2 tons could be obtained from an acre. Vegetables, including corn, beans, potatoes, beets, cabbage, onions, squash, and melons, brought $200 a ton; fruits and nuts, including apples, pears, peaches, figs, plums, nectarines, apricots, almonds, and walnuts, brought over $500 a ton. A few ranchers had vineyards and made wine. Vine cuttings were brought by Yount from Las Vegas in his saddlebags. He had 2-1/2 acres in seven varieties of grapes, and his Chateau Manse was said to have been superior to "California's finest" (Lingenfelter, 1986:169). Yount raised chickens, turkeys, ducks, and geese; he also had a sawmill in the Charleston Mountains and hauled lumber to Manvel, Vanderbilt, Goodsprings, and Las Vegas.

The White family on the front porch of their home at the Manse Ranch, Pahrump Valley, around 1900. Left to right, Maude Yount White, Harsha White, and Della White, who later married O.J. Fisk.

San Bernadino County Museum – Fisk Collection

By Buckboard Through Pahrump

In 1886 Thomas W. Brooks traveled by buckboard from the Los Angeles area to Oasis Valley and the present site of Beatty, Nevada. On his trip, he passed through the Pahrump Valley. His descriptions of the Younts and the life they had built in the wilderness are the best known accounts of the valley at that time.

Brooks wrote, "with an untiring energy, and a blessing of good health, and judicious management," the Younts worked to make the Manse Ranch a grand success. He said, "A dear home, or one more luxuriously supplied, or more convenient, or happier, cannot be found" (Brooks, 1970:12). By 1886, the Younts had built the farm up to 320 acres, which Brooks stated were purchased from the state of Nevada. He described the Manse Ranch as an "Oasis":

> A fertile spot, ornamented with fragrant flowers, evergreens, and every useful product for the comfort and use of man and beast, orchards and vineyards, preserves, raisins and wine, turkeys, ducks, chickens, and geese to the number of 400, fish swimming ponds, large and long, which have 100 inches of warm water constantly flowing through them (Brooks, 1970:12).

Brooks was lavish with his appreciation for Mrs. Yount's accomplishments:

> Too much praise cannot be given the precious mother, Mrs. Yount, who has reared

five sons and five daughters here. And though the church, and the schoolhouse and the tick of the telegraph was far away from their oasis home, intelligence and cultivation are there, after nature's own design, and void of the superfluous vanity with which the masses are burdened (Brooks, 1970:13).

By that time, three of the Younts' five daughters were married, and Della May White, the Whites' youngest daughter, was still living at home. The children, Brooks noted, were to be sent to Pomona, California, to complete their education.

It was not without some difficulty, however, that Mrs. Yount adapted to the Pahrump Valley wilderness. Upon first arriving in the Pahrump Valley, she asked her husband, on behalf of her children, "Where are we? Where are our neighbors; the church; the schoolhouse and the post office?" Joseph Yount's answer reflected the stark realities of the Pahrump Valley wilderness:

> We are in Palorump [Pahrump] Valley, Nye County, Nevada, and Mr. Bennett, six miles distance, is our only neighbor, except that we consider the hundreds of roving Paiutes neighbors; and as to the church, the schoolhouse and the post office, I hardly know which is the nearest, the settlement on Kern river, the Mormon church at St. George, Utah, or San Bernardino, but it is about 250 miles to the nearest post office (Brooks, 1970:11-12).

A team of ten horses pulls wagon filled with lumber, Pahrump Valley, Nevada, around 1900.

San Bernardino County Museum – Fisk Collection

Della White Fisk, daughter of Harsha and Maude White, who owned the Manse Ranch until 1910. Della married O.J. Fisk, a mining man from the Mojave Desert area, and spent most of the remainder of her life in San Bernadino, California.

San Bernardino County Museum – Fisk Collection

(Below) Corral in front of the main house. Manse Ranch, Pahrump Valley, Nevada, around 1900.

San Bernardino County Museum – Fisk Collection

Left to right: Dick Lee, Bob Lee, Clara Lee, Dora Lee, all children of Philander and Sally "Mops" Lee, circa 1910. Mops is believed to be short for Moppitts, a word meaning old lady, or old woman, in Southern Paiute. Woman on right not identified.   Nye County Town History Project – Brown Collection

Philander Lee sitting in a buckboard with his daughter, Dora Lee Brown, probably around 1915. Probably photographed at Resting Spring Ranch, near Tecopa, California.

Nye County Town History Project – Brown Collection

The Lee Brothers

The Lee brothers were major figures in the history of the Pahrump Valley area. There were four brothers: Philander (Phi), Leander (Cub), Meander, and Salamander. Phi and Cub first came to the Pahrump area in the winter of 1874-1875 with a herd of cattle from the San Joaquin Valley. They staked out a spring in the Amargosa Valley. Phi Lee, Harry Spiller, and Billy Yount (a son of Joseph Yount) are credited with finding the giant deposit of white borax salts that they named Monte Blanco. This discovery, which occurred in 1882, followed Winters' finding of borax at Furnace Creek. Phi and his brother Cub found another borax mineral deposit the next year, later named the Lila C. Roughly 3 million tons of borates still remain in the Monte Blanco deposit. Phi Lee and his partners sold their interests in the Monte Blanco deposit. Cub Lee remained in the area and Phi used his share of the receipts from the sale of the Monte Blanco to purchase the Resting Spring Ranch, where he stayed until about 1915. He then moved to a site in the Charleston Mountains. Both men married Indian women. Phi's wife, Sally, was a Panamint and reported to be a sister of Hungry Bill and Panamint Tom, famous in their own right in the history of Death Valley.

Sally and Phi Lee's children included Dick and Bob, who were probably in their thirties and living on the Resting Spring Ranch when they went looking for the Lost Breyfogle mine, one of the legendary lost lodes in the Death Valley area. They hitched up their outfit and drove to Ash Meadows and then on to the Indian Pass area in the Funeral Mountains on the west side of the Amargosa Valley. There they camped and prospected in the vicinity for several days, finding nothing. That night, sitting in front of the campfire, they discussed where they should look next. As they talked, the evening star was hanging over the mountain to the west of them, twinkling.

Bob Lee said, "We never went up that mountain, we didn't check that out."

"Oh hell," Dick Lee said, "that's barren; you can tell by looking at it."

The star remained on Bob's mind, however, and he talked his brother into staying another

Model-A Ford belonging to Bob Lee. No one was allowed to sit in the front seat of the car with Lee because it was reserved for Lee's dog. Pictured here are Dora Lee Brown, Bob Lee's sister, and Margie Brown, Dora Lee Brown's granddaughter and daughter of Dora's son Steve Brown.

Nye County Town History Project – Brown Collection

Dora Lee Brown and her granddaughter at Dora's place on the Yount Ranch, Pahrump Valley, circa 1940.

Nye County Town History Project – Wiley Collection

day or two to explore the mountain. The next morning, within an hour after breakfast, they hit a "helluva rich streak" of gold. That discovery led to the founding of Lee Camp in the Funeral Mountains, and the brothers made a good deal of money. They took their money to Rhyolite, which was near enough to be visible from their camp. There they dressed in fancy clothes including stovepipe hats, played the stock market, and of course soon were broke (D. Lowe, 1988).

When Bob Lee was an old man, Deke Lowe, a long-time resident of the area, was talking to Lee at his ranch located in southern Pahrump Valley, which was in dilapidated condition—tin cans, piles of junk, and old car bodies were scattered about. Lowe looked at Lee and asked, "Don't you wish you had put some of that money away?" referring to the money he had made at Lee Camp.

Lee's short reply summarized the prospector's credo: "Well, you know," he said slowly. "I'd rather be a has-been than a never-was" (D. Lowe, 1988).

Fourth of July at the Manse Ranch

The Fourth of July was an important holiday on the American frontier. It was usually celebrated with much fanfare and enthusiasm by the residents of the half-dozen big ranches located in southern Nevada. Besides the Manse and Pahrump ranches in Pahrump Valley, there were the Indian Springs Ranch and the Kyle and Stewart ranches in the Las Vegas Valley.

On the Fourth of July 1894, the entire population of the Las Vegas Valley and, we may presume, Indian Springs and the Pahrump Valley, gathered to celebrate the nation's birth at the home of Harsha White on the Manse Ranch. More than 50 people are said to have come for the festivities, some from as far away as 100 miles, including Helen Stewart and her children from the Las Vegas Valley, and guests from Pioche. Guests began arriving on July 3. They were entertained with various amusements; a dance was held that evening; and after midnight the Fourth was welcomed in by the firing of pistols and an anvil salute.

Festivities on the Fourth involved exercises and egg races, rock races, foot races, and sack races. John Yount provided an exhibition of turning and jumping on the bar, and the guests roared with laughter at the antics of George Rose and Charles Grundy, who played clowns. Patriotic songs were sung and a second dance was held that evening. A feast catered by William

Believed to be the old Pahrump Store. Until a window was constructed to the left of the double doors, a post office was housed on the left side of the building's interior. Individuals pictured are not identified. The store was located on the Pahrump Ranch, Pahrump Valley, Nye County, Nevada. The picture is believed to date from before 1920. Woman may be Clara Lee, daughter of Philander Lee.

Nye County Town History Project – Brown Collection

Sollender helped keep spirits high. On July 5, the owners of the Pahrump Ranch, the MacArthurs, invited guests to adjourn to their ranch 6 miles away for an evening of enjoyment followed by dinner at 1:00 in the morning. Guests headed home on July 6 (Townley, 1974:4-5).

The Period of Elevated Expectations

The early years of the twentieth century formed a period of rising expectations in Nevada. Jim Butler's discovery of silver at Tonopah had, for all intents and purposes, saved the state after a precipitous decline in mineral production and population from 1880 to 1900. Harry Stimler's discovery at Goldfield in 1902, followed by the discovery by Shorty Harris and Ed Cross at Bullfrog in 1904, added impetus to the new economic boom started at Tonopah. Senator Clark's purchase of the Stewart Ranch in the Las Vegas Valley, his construction of the SP, LA & SL Railroad, and the construction of railroads to the north by Senator Clark and Borax Smith, linking Tonopah with Las Vegas and the Santa Fe Railroad at Ludlow, California, provided further optimism about the economic future of southern Nevada.

The Pahrump Valley was perhaps the most isolated community in the region, with neither good roads nor a railroad; nevertheless, there was great enthusiasm for the valley's future based on the large tracts of land suitable for agriculture, a relatively long growing season, and seemingly endless quantities of artesian water.

Team and freight wagons, Manse Ranch, Pahrump Valley, circa 1910. Note the sign on the building in the background that reads "Buy Lots in Johnnie Now." Nye County Town History Project – Brown Collection

At least two groups of colonists seemed to be interested in settling in the Pahrump Valley. The first effort, some years prior to 1905, was by individuals, described as "tenderfeet," from the eastern United States; it apparently was a failure. Little is known of this effort. In 1905 there was a flurry of activity among a group of southern Californians who planned to form a colony in the Pahrump Valley. This effort was sponsored by borax king and builder of the Tonopah and Tidewater Railroad, Borax Smith, and railroad titan E. H. Harriman. The purpose of the plan was to stimulate business for the railroad, but, like the earlier colonization plan, it was a failure. Efforts to place a large population in the Pahrump Valley would have to wait another 60 years.

By 1905 both the Manse and the Pahrump ranches were productive enterprises and were known as resorts for weary desert travelers. Trees provided shade in the hottest months, the finest of vegetables and fruits were grown, and their springs provided water for swimming and relaxation. Many varieties of trees grew on the Manse Ranch including willows, cottonwoods, poplars, and fruit and nut trees, such as walnuts, apples, peaches, pears, and plums; umbrella trees were clustered around the ranch house. Several varieties of grapes continued to flourish. Mining activity throughout the southern Nevada and Death Valley areas, especially at Rhyolite and Beatty, provided ready markets for the ranches' products; Harsha White is reported to have made $10,000 in one year on hay and meat shortly before 1905.

In 1910, Harsha White sold the Manse Ranch for $50,000. At that time the property consisted of 760 acres, 300 of which were under cultivation in orchards, grains, and alfalfa. White also owned 400 acres of valuable timber land in the Charleston Mountains, which were included in the sale. Purchasers of the ranch were Hoffman and Vetter of Redondo, California. Joseph Yount died in 1907, and Mrs. Yount died in 1912 in San Bernardino.

Buildings at the Manse Ranch, Pahrump Valley, Nevada, around 1900.

San Bernardino County Museum – Fisk Collection

Wagons filled with hay pulled by a string of twelve horses and mules. Pahrump Valley, Nevada, around 1900.

San Bernardino County Museum – Fisk Collection

Lawless Country

The Pahrump Valley was more than 160 miles from the county seat at Tonopah, and it remained quite isolated from other communities for many decades. It shared with Ash Meadows a reputation for lawlessness. Groups and individuals tended to deal with illegal and criminal acts in their own way.

In 1910, Harsha White told of an incident that had occurred about 30 years previously, which illustrates how miners and ranchers in Pahrump tended to settle disputes. It seems some local Indians had been stealing and killing ranchers' livestock. Growing tired of the Indians' behavior, the settlers and miners were determined to put a stop to it; the methods they used would be extremely controversial today, to say the least. Ranchers and miners held a meeting at Ivanpah and notified the Indians that those guilty of stealing and killing stock must be brought to justice. To secure this end, they held two Southern Paiute hostage and sent word to the relatives of the hostages that the perpetrators of the crimes must be caught and punished or the lives of the hostages would be "sacrificed."

Not wishing the deaths of the innocent hostages, a band of Indian trackers set out on the trail of the criminals, two men named Panquitch and Horseshutem. (Horseshutem had been implicated in the 1876 killing of Joseph Yount's draft horses.) The criminals were tracked over many miles of desert and Panquitch was cornered at the Wilson Ranch west of Las Vegas. One Indian caught and pinned Panquitch's arms and another picked up an ax and split open his skull. The Wilsons, owners of the ranch and themselves part Indian, were called as witnesses to the act and proof of Panquitch's death was sent back to Ivanpah. The Indian posse then

Leaf from an unknown book featuring a picture of an unidentified individual in front of the Pahrump Store, Pahrump. Date unknown.

Nye County Town History Project – Goodson Collection

Front page of *Las Vegas Evening Review and Journal*, January 22, 1931.

picked up the trail of Horseshutem. A long chase ensued, and after several days he was finally overtaken near Tybo, Nevada, more than 250 miles from the scene of his crimes. Horseshutem was shot in the back; proof of his death was sent back to Ivanpah, whereupon the innocent hostages were released. The killing and stealing of stock by Indians were said to have ceased thereafter.

Frontier justice in Pahrump produced a number of shootings and killings. In 1910, one killing led to worries about a possible Indian uprising. Joe Lake, a white man, killed Charlie Tecopa, son of Chief Tecopa, at the Manse Ranch. The cause of the trouble was not determined, but Lake claimed that the Indian had opened fire on him first. A coroner was summoned from Beatty by whites and news of the killing quickly spread among the local Indians. Tecopa was the last surviving chief of the Tecopa "royal" family and the Indians were outraged. They gathered in the vicinity of the Manse Ranch and threatened action, vowing vengeance on the slayer. Two days later, thirty Indians were camped at the ranch; they refused to allow officers to take Lake to Amargosa, stating that it was their right to "mete out justice according to their own standards." Ranchers guarded the prisoner closely for the next two days. Finally, on the fifth day, the prisoner was smuggled to Johnnie under cover of darkness and taken to Goldfield.

Old-timers in the valley say there was always some kind of feud or personal grudge precipitating violence in the community. Deke Lowe told of the murder of the Manse Ranch owner in the 1920s. The victim, a Mr. Kazarang, had a reputation for being stingy. Lowe cited, as an example of his tightfistedness, how a lavish meal could be obtained at the cafe in Shoshone for 50 cents, yet Kazarang, a person of some means, would sit outside the restaurant beside his parked car and eat cheese and crackers rather than buy a meal. A ranch employee became embroiled with Kazarang in a dispute over wages, contending that the rancher was shorting him. The worker vowed vengeance. Not long afterward, Kazarang was found dead in his pigpen, where the pigs had chewed on him. An investigation revealed that the hired hand had shot the owner, put a rope around him, and dragged him into the pigpen. The employee was arrested, tried in Tonopah, and found guilty, but he received a light sentence because everyone in the area was aware of the owner's stinginess and his tendency to cheat people.

There was a tradition in the Pahrump area of being on the margin of the law, so it is not surprising that residents tended to ignore the prohibition laws of the 1920s and early 1930s. The valley was the site of considerable production of illegal alcohol. As might be expected, such activity sometimes led to violence. One case involved a deadly confrontation between Joe L. Hudson, a local trapper, and "Tank" Sharp, a man of quarter-Indian descent, at Hidden Ranch, John Yount's property south of the Manse Ranch. Sharp, it seems, had been drinking all afternoon, though he was not drunk. Hudson arrived about 9:00 that evening, and Sharp immediately accused him of being one of "those damn prohis who put me out of a job." Throughout the evening, Sharp insisted that Hudson was a "prohi" and was implicated in the raid on stills in the area a few days earlier. Sharp vowed vengeance, yet John Yount seemed to have succeeded in persuading him to go to bed. Hudson was invited to spend the rest of the night at the ranch. About midnight, Hudson stepped out of the house to drain the radiator of his car. As he walked out, Hudson was narrowly missed by a shot. He ran to his car and grabbed his rifle from the front seat. In the darkness, he heard the words, "You damn prohi, I'll get you now."

As Hudson stepped around the car, he met a "human being" with a gun and opened fire. "I let him have it before he could get me," he later explained. Sharp was found shot in the chest; he never regained consciousness and died in less than half an hour. Richard Lee, Mrs. Lee, and Yount got in the car to drive to Goodsprings to notify the authorities, but the car broke down and Lee was forced to walk 30 miles into Goodsprings. An investigation proved that Sharp did run a still and a jury found that Hudson had shot in self-defense.

But the story does not end there. We now know that Pahrump Indians considered Joe L. Hudson to be a "mean" man. Many whites in the community did not think much better, considering him a "no good." In the fall of 1935, Hudson was living in a small house by a spring near the southeast margin of the Pahrump Ranch. A number of Indians lived in the vicinity, including Oscar Bruce, a Southern Paiute from Pahrump, who lived about one quarter mile away from Hudson. Hudson's killing of "Tank" Sharp probably remained in the local Indians' memory. Once again Hudson became embroiled in violence with a local Indian, but this time the outcome was different.

It started when Jim Steve, a Navajo living in Pahrump, approached Hudson's house on foot. It is unknown why he did so; perhaps the two had had a disagreement. Unexpectedly, Hudson drew down on Steve with his rifle and shot him. It may be that having killed one Indian without punishment, Hudson supposed he could get away with such an act again. Steve fell wounded, seemingly dead. Jim Steve's children either witnessed the event or quickly heard of it. Alarmed, they ran to Oscar Bruce's house for help. Bruce wasted no time in reacting. He grabbed his rifle and headed for Hudson's place. Rather than approach from the front, as Steve had done, Bruce snuck up from the back, and slipped around the side of the building to the front where, through an open window, he saw Hudson. Bruce stuck his rifle through the window and killed Hudson instantly. About the same time, Bruce and the others learned that Jim Steve was not dead, but had only been knocked out from a shot across the forehead.

Rosie Arnold, a relative of Oscar Bruce, was at Judge Kimball's house in Beatty when the sheriff's deputy for southern Nye County, Vic Vignolo, arrived to pick up Kimball to accompany him to Pahrump to investigate the murder. Hours later she was still at Kimball's house when the judge arrived home before taking Bruce to jail in Tonopah. She remembered looking out the window of the judge's house and seeing her relative in custody in the back seat of the deputy's car. The next day Rosie and her mother, Annie Beck, rode on horseback to Pahrump to see the site of the crime their relative had committed. She remembered how the wall of the room was splattered with Hudson's blood. Oscar Bruce was tried and convicted in Tonopah, but only served about a year in the state penitentiary in Carson City. Hudson's bad reputation was seen to have been an important factor in the relatively light sentence.

Such stories are more than isolated incidents. Virtually anyone who spent more than a short period of time in Pahrump in the period before World War II can recall numerous acts of violence and frontier justice.

The efficient linking of Pahrump with the outside world through modern highways and communication systems, along with the use of modern police and judicial methods, has put an end to a law enforcement system that resembled the rough and ready ways of the frontier. These changes have stopped individuals from taking the law into their own hands through revenge and personal vendettas. But these practices remain a part of Pahrump's colorful past.

The Pahrump Economy in the 1930s

By the early 1930s the agricultural potential of the Pahrump Valley was legendary, yet the valley remained relatively undeveloped. Although it was estimated to have three-fourths of the available water to be found in the Moapa Valley, there was no comparable community growth. A report prepared by the University of Nevada took note of this disparity and listed several reasons why Pahrump lagged behind Moapa (Venstrom, 1932:81). The reasons tended to have to do with (1) a difference in surface water, with more water being on the surface in the Moapa Valley; and (2) the greater isolation of the Pahrump Valley, with consequent difficulties in transporting produce to markets.

A Dude Ranch

Despite the lack of development and the tiny population, there was no shortage of ideas for using the valley's abundant resources. Following the passage of laws in the spring of 1931 legalizing gaming and reducing the residency requirement for a Nevada divorce from three months to six weeks, dude ranches sprang up in many areas of the state for people who wished to establish their residency for divorce in a more bucolic setting. These ranches were especially prevalent in the Reno and Las Vegas areas, and some, such as the old Kyle Ranch in North Las Vegas, were very popular.

The idea seemed sound, and an effort was made to create such an enterprise in Pahrump. It was known as the Pahrump Valley Dude Ranch and was located at the Pahrump Ranch. It operated during the mid-1930s and was run by Lois Deimel and her husband, Ed. The Deimels, easterners of considerable means, were friends of Isadore Dockweiler, one of the principals in the Pahrump Land Company, which owned the Pahrump Ranch at that time. The Deimels had learned of the ranch through him, and they moved to Pahrump's dry climate because Ed suffered from tuberculosis.

Many guests came from southern California, but some were from as far away as New York City. A fieldstone swimming pool was constructed close to one of the large springs, but there was little other investment in new facilities. As a business, the dude ranch did not last long. Throughout, the Pahrump Ranch remained a working operation.

Meanwhile, the other major property in the valley changed hands. In 1936 Dr. H. D. Cornell, a nose and throat specialist from San Diego, California, purchased the Manse Ranch and took immediate possession.

Edmund L. Fleming, southern Nevada educator, who taught school in the Pahrump Valley in the late 1930s and Gertie Case Buol, Pop Buol's daughter-in-law, salute Chateau Buol wine produced by Buol at his Pahrump Valley winery, 1938-1939.

Nye County Town History Project – Fleming Collection

CHAPTER THREE

People of the Pahrump Valley

T he history of the Pahrump Valley in the 1930s and 1940s is the story of several very different people, some of whom moved into the area to have the freedom to live highly individual lifestyles. The valley remained undeveloped, with virtually no institutional base or infrastructure. But in a sense it was already rich in its tradition of allowing people to work the land, remain independent, and not be typecast into neat molds or categories.

Frank "Pop" Buol's Winery and Store

Frank "Pop" Buol was brother of Peter Buol, who was the first mayor of Las Vegas. He settled in the Pahrump Valley during the early 1900s. It is quite possible that he entered southern Nevada as a surveyor, sent to the area to survey the Spring Mountain Range for timber. After completing his job in the Spring Mountains, he might have walked into the Pahrump Valley, finding a place where he wanted to spend the rest of his life. He drilled one of the first wells in the valley and had a small farm with numerous fruit trees and a vineyard.

He did not raise alfalfa or grain on his property and did not keep livestock, aside from an occasional pig, which he would let run through his orchard to clean up fruit that had dropped off the trees. Then in the fall he would butcher the pig.

Buol was most famous for the wine he produced; he is said to have had either the first or second licensed winery in the state of Nevada. He produced about 1100 gallons a year, and he supplied his vintage to the Biltmore Hotel in Los Angeles. Buol maintained a regular, fully equipped winery on his property, and it was still intact (although nonoperative) in 1989. He had little wine cellars dug into the sand hills around his property, in which he stored barrels of wine. Years after the ranch was sold, bulldozers were used to level some of the sand hills and workers discovered the stored barrels; some caches may still exist. He told valley residents that he drank a quart of wine a day. Whenever Buol had guests, he would break out the bottle, saving his better wines for those whom he particularly liked.

For several decades, Pop Buol ran a small store on his property, which he closed about 1946.

Two young women at the Pahrump Ranch, all dressed up with no place to go. At left is Beryl Hughes, daughter of Pahrump Ranch owner John R. Hughes; at right is Mabel Ishmael, daughter of well-known Nye County resident George Ishmael. Photo was taken circa 1938, when Beryl Hughes was 15 and Mabel Ishmael was 16. Beryl Hughes later became a model in Los Angeles.

Nye County Town History Project – Hughes Collection

He continued on in Pahrump for several years after the store was closed, but moved to Tonopah in the mid-1950s to be with relatives. The property was later purchased by Doby Doc Caudill.

John R. Hughes Plants Cotton

The first cotton grown in the Pahrump Valley may have been planted near the valley's springs 1000 or more years ago by Anasazi Indians; the Southern Paiute may also have experimented with it. It is known that in 1917 the Pahrump Valley Company, owner of the Pahrump Ranch, announced its intention to plant 200 acres of cotton on the ranch the next spring; but the results of this effort are unknown.

The first well-documented effort at growing cotton in the Pahrump Valley began in 1936. John R. Hughes from Porterville, California, moved onto the Pahrump Ranch with his wife and children. Hughes first heard about Pahrump from friends in Porterville, California, who sometimes hauled cattle and sheep out of the Pahrump Valley. They told stories of large amounts of available land, cheap water, and a relatively mild climate. Their stories aroused his interest and Hughes drove to Pahrump to see for himself.

Hughes and his associates purchased the 11,920-acre Pahrump Ranch for $135,000 from the Pahrump Valley Company, headed by Isadore B. Dockweiler and associates, including Paul Shoup of the Board of Directors of the Southern Pacific Railroad, and Jack Shoup, an agent for Associated Oil Company. Dockweiler and his associates had held the ranch since the early 1900s, perhaps as a diversion and tax write-off. Much of the enlargement and consolidation of the ranch took place under the Pahrump Valley Company.

Betty Jean Hughes, daughter of Pahrump Ranch owner John R. Hughes, sitting on a calf on the Pahrump Ranch, about 1938.   Nye County Town History Project – Hughes Collection

Leon Hughes, one of John Hughes' sons, was a teenager when the family moved to the Pahrump Valley. When asked to recall what the valley looked like in 1936, Hughes described it:

> Well, the only way I'd know to describe it, is if you'd go out to one of these mesquite thickets where you can't see any buildings or anything; that's what the whole thing looked like. There was nothing here. There were 3 or 4 buildings on the Manse Ranch, a lot of buildings on the Pahrump Ranch, 1 or 2 on the Raycraft Ranch, Frank Buol had a little winery, but there was absolutely nothing here. There weren't over 20 people; there were a lot more Indians than white people (Hughes, 1988).

Hughes recalled two stores in the valley. One, at Frank Buol's place, carried a few canned goods and staples such as flour, but no perishables. Buol's store was really more of an emergency food source than anything else; it was mostly patronized by prospectors, who were fairly numerous in the hills at that time, with a fair amount of activity at Johnnie. The other store, located on the Pahrump Ranch, was operated by Ed Deimel. It was said to have originally been a saloon, and it dated back to before the turn of the century.

Betty Jean Hughes, daughter of John R. Hughes, riding her brother Leon's horse, Chico, on the Pahrump Ranch about 1938. The fence in the background encircled the "motel."

Nye County Town History Project – Hughes Collection

Social life in the valley was scant and people lived in isolation. Hughes recalled four or five families living on the Pahrump Ranch, two families on the Manse, one on the Raycraft Ranch, and Frank Buol. There were also one or two "homesteaders" in the valley who had very small operations. The valley had a small school with one teacher. Ed Fleming was the teacher for two years beginning in 1938 and he had fourteen students—four Indians and ten whites. The Rose School District paid him $1800 a year, and he took his meals with Pop Buol.

When John R. Hughes took over the Pahrump Ranch in 1936, he continued to plant 200 or 300 acres of grain and alfalfa. In the spring of 1937 he planted about 600 acres of cotton. The results were both enlightening and devastating, and, for all intents and purposes, bankrupted Hughes. He had planted most of his cotton on newly cleared, virgin land, but he also planted a small amount on land that had been in alfalfa. He found that the cotton planted on virgin ground did not thrive, but that cotton planted where alfalfa had been growing produced abundantly. The virgin soil had salt in it and very little humus; it took an alfalfa crop or a grain crop a couple of years to leach out some of the salt and set a little humus in the soil for the deeper-rooted cotton plants. Once this had been done, cotton plants grew vigorously. Unfortunately Hughes learned that lesson too late. He had expended most of his bankroll in planting the first cotton crop. He lost the Pahrump Ranch, which returned to Dockweiler and associates.

Leon Hughes, son of John R. Hughes, on the Pahrump Ranch, 1938. John Hughes was then the owner of the ranch.

Nye County Town History Project – Hughes Collection

(Below) Cowboys branding a calf on the Manse Ranch, probably in the 1940s.

Nye County Town History Project – Ford Collection

(Left) Lois Kellogg beside her prize heifer on Arlemont Ranch in Fish Lake Valley, circa 1940.
Denny Lynch

(Right) Lois Kellogg as a young woman with one of her Russian wolfhounds.
Nye County Town History Project – Hafen Collection

Lois Kellogg: Easterner Turned Rancher

Lois Kellogg was a woman of considerable wealth. She grew up in the East, rebelled against her family, and moved to Palm Springs, California. Finding Palm Springs too confining, she purchased the Arlemont Ranch in Fish Lake Valley in Esmeralda County; later, in 1939, she purchased a large block of land in the south end of the Pahrump Valley adjoining the Manse Ranch, which came to be known as the Kellogg Ranch.

Kellogg was interested in growing barley and hay and raising cattle on her Pahrump property. She drilled some of the best wells in the valley. Long-time residents recall that when she brought in her first artesian well, water shot nearly 50 feet in the air because of the tremendous pressure. She installed, at some considerable expense, a facility for rolling barley grain. She was then in her mid 40s, and though a small woman, she would truck cattle raised on her property to Los Angeles alone, over dirt roads as far as Baker. She would sleep in the truck or in the open air beside the truck in her bedroll.

Lois Kellogg died before the farm became really productive. (Productivity may have not been her goal, however. Harry Ford recalled one crop of barley that was never harvested because Kellogg found the standing grain so beautiful.) There are slightly varying versions of her death, but all agree that she raised Russian wolfhound dogs that she loved—she had more than 50 at her Fish Lake Valley residence—and that the dogs passed tularemia to her, perhaps through a bite.

Stanley Ford and Dairy Cattle

Stanley Ford was born in Wisconsin in 1902 to a family of dairy farmers who had homesteaded in that state. The cold Wisconsin winters did not agree with Ford, and in 1925 he loaded his wife and daughter into an old Model-T Ford and moved to southern California. In

House on the Raycraft Ranch, 1945, looking west. The house was built by Jim Raycraft from lumber obtained at the Johnnie Townsite and hauled down to Pahrump in wagons. The car is a 1931 Graham, used by Stanley Ford to haul mail to Pahrump from the Johnnie Siding on the Tonopah highway. It is said that during the summer the house was mostly hidden by the large willow trees.

Nye County Town History Project – Ford Collection

1944 he heard about the Pahrump Valley and its abundant artesian waters, and he moved there. Initially he located on property now known as the Basin Ranch, but when wells being drilled did not prove out, he located on the Raycraft Ranch, where he spent the next eight years.

Ford and his family moved onto the Raycraft place as sharecroppers, and he supplemented his income by hauling mail from the Johnnie Siding once a week for delivery in Pahrump. The Fords always kept dairy cattle, and though it was illegal during World War II, they sold butter in Shoshone and Tecopa, sometimes as much as 100 pounds a month, for as much as $1 a pound. The market was good in that area because the big Noonday lead mine and area talc mines were in operation. Mrs. Ford hand-churned the butter. At first Ford milked by hand, then purchased a David-Bradley milking machine with a gasoline-powered vacuum pump. Milk was also run through a hand-operated separator, and cream was hauled to the Rancho Grande Creamery in Las Vegas, where sweet cream brought a higher price than sour cream. They also raised chickens and turkeys for market.

Life on the Raycraft property involved hard work from sunup till sundown. Horse-drawn farming equipment was used to produce hay for the dairy cattle and grain for the chickens and turkeys. Work with the livestock and in the fields was primarily the responsibility of Mr. Ford. The women's hard duties included laundry on one day a week and ironing on another. Mrs. Ford washed with a gas-powered washing machine. She always helped milk the cows and processed the cream in the cookshack.

The community was still small at this time and the cooperation among residents so evident during the early days was still strong. People worked together and helped each other out. At least once a week, someone would go to town to purchase groceries, and they would always shop for others in the community. People enjoyed each other and liked to get together.

Stanley Ford was a jack-of-all-trades and in addition to his duties as a farmer, he drilled wells and was also the valley barber. He had a barber chair and hand clippers and every three or four weeks he and his family, with other valley residents, would be invited to one home,

Looking west from the Raycraft Ranch, Pahrump Valley, Nye County, Nevada, around 1944. Cedar posts, on the left, were cut in the Spring Mountain Range. Pictured is a four-wheel trailer constructed by Stanley Ford.

Nye County Town History Project – Ford Collection

Stanley Ford operating the controls of his well-drilling equipment in the Pahrump Valley.

Nye County Town History Project – Ford Collection

Well-drilling rig owned and operated by Stanley Ford. During the 1940s and 1950s Ford drilled many of the wells in the Pahrump Valley.

Nye County Town History Project – Ford Collection

Eighteen-year-old Harry "Button" Ford and his 1946 Ford convertible, parked in front of his home in Pahrump Valley, during the summer of 1955.   Nye County Town History Project – Ford Collection

usually the Pahrump Ranch or the Manse Ranch. Ford would take his barber chair and clippers along and spend the day cutting people's hair. Guests would bring a dish or pie or cake and everyone would enjoy a pot-luck dinner.

As Ford's son Harry grew, he was expected to help his father with work on the farm. Yet childhood on the farm was a special world, which included swimming in the springs and hunting with his .22 rifle, for which he paid $8 and for which his mother allowed him one shell a day. There were ducks on the ponds and rabbits and quail year round, and no game wardens. The ponds held frogs, tadpoles, and carp 2 feet long. The children used to reach back into holes under the banks in the ponds and streams and grab fish by hand. "Anything that wiggled, you grabbed it," Harry Ford remembered. "When you got hold of a fish 12 inches long, he really put up a fight" (Ford, 1988). A special treat was to sneak over to the Pahrump Ranch where the ponds were larger and the adventures even more attractive. Ford recalled that there was usually a white boy or two to play with, but most of his pals were Indian children.

Roland Wiley and the Hidden Hills Ranch

For many years one of the largest holdings of private land in the Pahrump Valley has been the Hidden Hills Ranch, which straddles the Nevada-California border near the highway linking the Pahrump Valley with the Resting Spring Ranch and Tecopa, California. At present, about 1250 acres of the ranch are located in Nevada; the rest are in California. A vast parcel of land, at one time encompassing nearly 18,000 acres but more recently 14,400 acres, Hidden Hills Ranch has for many years been under the control of Roland Wiley, a Las Vegas attorney.

Wiley was born in Iowa in 1904, attended school in Iowa and the University of Wisconsin, and was graduated from George Washington University in Washington, D.C., where he obtained a law degree in 1927. Soon after graduation he traveled to California to visit relatives and stopped in Las Vegas. Because of his time spent in Washington, Wiley was familiar with federal government plans to construct Boulder Dam near Las Vegas. Although construction had not begun, he recognized that the giant project would stimulate growth in the small city. He moved to Las Vegas and became a member of the Nevada bar, serving a term as Clark County district attorney when the Las Vegas strip was being developed.

Although Wiley had numerous opportunities to make major investments in real estate in the Las Vegas Valley, which would have paid off in staggering profits, he long ago demonstrated a penchant for real estate investments in the Pahrump Valley. Wiley explained:

> I never liked the Las Vegas Valley, because it was hard pan and sandy gravel, and over in the Pahrump Valley, it's all good American soil, you know, agricultural soil. Being an Iowa farm boy, why, I put more value to that land; less value here [Las Vegas] (Wiley, 1988).

Wiley became involved in the Pahrump Valley through his efforts to settle the estate of John Yount, son of pioneer Joseph Yount. For several years, John lived with a woman who became known as Belle Yount. John and Belle, it seemed, had always intended to get married, but somehow never did. When John died in the early 1930s, heirs in the Redlands and Riverside areas of California hired a lawyer, Frank McNamee, to represent their interests. Belle Yount came to Wiley and asked him to determine whether she was Yount's common-law wife. When Wiley asked Belle why she had never married John, she replied, "Well, we went to town many times to get married, but we always ended up at a bawdy house and got drunk" (Wiley, 1988).

His efforts to determine Belle Yount's marital status first took Wiley to Pahrump Valley. The trip took 3-1/2 hours and necessitated driving to Goodsprings, then through Mesquite Valley, as it was then called (it is now known as Sandy Valley), then north into the Pahrump Valley to the Hidden Hills Ranch, then known as the Hidden Ranch of John Yount. (Travel to the Hidden Hills Ranch up Highway 95 through Indian Springs then took 4-1/2 hours.) Wiley recalled that, at the time, about 1939, the Manse Ranch was vacant and under foreclosure on a $15,000 note, and the Pahrump Ranch could have been purchased a short time later for $100,000.

After an investigation, Wiley could not establish Belle's status as a common-law wife, and he advised her to buy out the interests of the other heirs. She followed his advice, but it was clear to Wiley that Belle did not want the ranch. She suggested that Wiley buy the property, and he did so.

Over the years, the Wiley trust expanded its holdings in the valley. Although the holdings diminished somewhat (he sold parcels to Preferred Equities and others in the 1970s), in 1989 the Wiley trust was by far the largest private land holder in the valley, and the property represented an immense source of future land and community development.

Wiley has used his holdings in the Pahrump Valley as a refuge from the hustle and stress of city life as well as an investment. His status as a true desert individualist becomes most evident in his work on his Cathedral Canyon. A short distance from his home at the Hidden Hills Ranch, just off the Tecopa highway, Wiley modified a lovely canyon, which ranges from a few to 200 to 300 feet

Sam Yount (circa 1900), brother of John who founded the Hidden (Hills) Ranch in the southern part of the Pahrump Valley around 1900. Sam and John were sons of Joseph and Margaret Yount.

San Bernardino County Museum – Fisk Collection

John Yount's home on the Hidden Ranch, now known as the Hidden Hills Ranch, Pahrump Valley, about 1917. Located off to the right of this photograph was a windmill and a blacksmith shop.

Nye County Town History Project – Brown Collection

House located on the Hidden Hills Ranch, southern Pahrump Valley, 1940s. Originally constructed by John Yount, the building has been improved and occupied since the 1930s by Roland Wiley.

San Bernardino County Museum – Fisk Collection

wide and perhaps 50 to 60 feet deep, as an artist would use paint and canvas to express his personal vision of life and nature. He constructed a trail up the canyon, along which are chairs and benches for people to use as they stop and contemplate the surroundings. Statues and other works of art have been placed along the trail and in niches on the cliffs. Along the trail are signboards with quotes and poems expressing Wiley's philosophy of life and advice for living, both religious and secular. A 200-foot suspension bridge spans the canyon; the site is wired throughout and is lighted every night—the best time to see the attraction, so close to Las Vegas, but visually so different. Wiley bears the expense for the entire project and admission is free. Cathedral Canyon is a special place for the humanity it expresses and for the philosophy of a longtime Pahrump Valley resident. The Old Spanish Trail connecting Mountain Springs with Stump Springs is visible near the head of Cathedral Canyon; Stump Springs is only 3 miles from the canyon.

Suspension bridge above Cathedral Canyon constructed by Roland Wiley in 1972. Hidden Hills Ranch, Pahrump Valley.

Nye County Town History Project – Wiley Collection

Cathedral Canyon was created by Roland Wiley to express his philosophy of life.

Nye County Town History Project – Wiley Collection

Visitors at the Hidden Hills Ranch during the 1950s. Hoot Gibson is standing behind the hitching post shaking hands with Murdell Earl, owner of the ENT Drug Store in North Las Vegas.

Nye County Town History Project – Wiley Collection

Cabins on the Hidden Hills Ranch, Pahrump Valley, 1950s.

San Bernardino County Museum – Fisk Collection

Roland Wiley, left, and Elmer Bowman, owner of the Manse Ranch, far right, visiting an Indian family who lived in a cottage on the Manse Ranch, circa 1950.   Nye County Town History Project – Wiley Collection

The Bowman Family Improves Manse Ranch

Dr. H. D. Cornell, a southern California physician, purchased the Manse Ranch in the late 1930s after it had been abandoned for a time. The ranch's abandonment was probably related to the economy and the lack of readily available markets following closure of the mines in the Pahrump region. Cornell purchased the ranch, consisting of 2000 acres, for approximately $20,000. While he owned it, he expanded his holdings to 6700 acres, mainly by buying the Kellogg Ranch. In 1946 Elmer S. Bowman bought the Manse Ranch from Cornell.

Elmer Bowman came from a pioneering family in Moapa; he was involved in a number of business ventures there. By the early 1930s he was in the dairy business, providing milk for Las Vegas, where construction of Boulder Dam had begun. At the age of 19, Perry, Bowman's older son, established his own dairy in the Moapa Valley. But times were not easy. By the early 1940s, land in the valley had been split into small parcels, which made it difficult for a farmer to get a unit large enough to work.

Elmer Bowman decided to leave Moapa and move to Pahrump, where plenty of land and water were available and where he could establish a large dairy. Bowman talked his son Perry and two daughters and sons-in-law (the Frehner and Christensen families) into moving to Pahrump with him. At first the acreage was operated as one large family farm, but gradually portions were split off as various family members went their own way.

The Bowmans' first years in the valley were not easy. "Pahrump was very tough," Perry Bowman remembered (Bowman, 1988). When they moved there, it had been years since any farming activities had been fully successful. Out-of-state money often subsidized operations. Still, Elmer Bowman and his family persevered and quickly improved their property, constructing several new homes and outbuildings and bringing virgin land into cultivation.

In the 1920s, the Automobile Club of Southern California installed road signs in the Pahrump Valley to assist travelers who might become lost on the many dirt roads that crisscrossed the barren desert valley. Travelers coming from California had no way of knowing when they had crossed the border and had entered Nevada. John Yount's Hidden Ranch was only 1.5 miles inside the Nevada line. Photo taken about 1936.

Nye County Town History Project – Wiley Collection

Elmer Bowman (left) and Roland Wiley are pictured in a cotton field on the Manse Ranch, owned by Elmer Bowman, early 1950s.   Nye County Town History Project – Wiley Collection

Bowman and other Mormons had a slight farming advantage over farmers who arrived later from California because agricultural techniques and practices that worked in Moapa generally seemed to be more effective in Pahrump than practices common in the San Joaquin and Imperial valleys in California.

Elmer Bowman became a community leader, was active in the improvement of the educational system in Pahrump, and worked with state and local leaders to modernize the valley. He was instrumental in initiating Mormon Church services, which in the early years were held in worshippers' homes. Later services were held in the congregation's own church, the first constructed in the valley. Much of the Bowmans' social life during the early years focused around church activities.

Tim Hafen: Modern Pioneer in Cotton and Alfalfa

The 1950s and 1960s were decades of general prosperity for American agriculture. Farmers in southern Nevada and Utah and the Central Valley of California were looking for places to expand. Because of its isolation, the Pahrump Valley was one of the few areas in the west where large quantities of arable virgin land could still be found. Further, cotton was bringing good prices in the 1950s; and since Leon Hughes had demonstrated conclusively in 1948 that cotton could be grown profitably in the Pahrump Valley, cheap land and abundant water made it almost certain that farmers from other areas in southern Nevada and the Central Valley in

Cotton fields belonging to Tim Hafen, Pahrump, Nevada, 1970s. Mt. Charleston is in the background.

Nye County Town History Project – Hafen Collection

Cotton Becomes King in Pahrump

Leon Hughes never forgot his father's efforts to grow cotton in Pahrump Valley. Although the family had returned to Porterville after the failure to make the Pahrump Ranch pay, Leon returned to Pahrump in 1948 to try again. There was "something about Pahrump that got into my blood, and I didn't want to leave," Hughes explained. He and his partner, Vern Schwartz, rented 120 acres from Elmer Bowman. "What are you going to do with it [the rented land]?" Elmer Bowman asked Hughes in 1948.

"I'm going to grow cotton," Hughes replied.

"Do you think you can grow cotton here?" Bowman asked.

"I know damn well I can, if I get a chance," Hughes answered (Hughes, 1988).

Hughes knew cotton would grow well in the right soil; he had seen his father do it. And, indeed, he produced cotton crops in 1948 and 1949. The crops were quite good and his success demonstrated to others that the Pahrump Valley could be productive in cotton. In a short period of time, most of the ranchers and farmers in the valley began growing cotton, at least as part of their acreage. The era that began in 1948 and lasted until about 1970 was described by Perry Bowman as "the golden agricultural period of Pahrump Valley" (Bowman, 1988).

Shortly after he began successfully growing cotton in the valley, Hughes became associated with another innovation residents still speak of proudly. He picked his first crop with mechanical cotton pickers, but it had to be trucked to California for ginning because there was no gin in the valley. Ordinarily cotton is loosely packed in cotton wagons and the wagons are towed to the gin. It would have been highly impractical to transport the cotton to California in such wagons, and ranchers found that when they tried to pack the cotton loosely on a truck it was impossible to get a load that would make the trip worthwhile. Hughes devised a system whereby cotton would be fed into a hay baler, compressed and packed, and then tied; the heavy bales would then be trucked to the cotton gin. Some feared that such packing would ruin the cotton, causing it to get hot and spoil, reducing its grade and the price a farmer could obtain for it. But experience proved just the opposite; compacting the cotton did not reduce the cotton's quality—if anything, it enhanced it.

One-row cotton picker in a cotton field,
Hafen Farms, Pahrump Valley, circa 1958.

Central Nevada Historical Society –
Jacobson Collection

(Right) Mechanical cotton picker
operated by Perry Bowman,
Pahrump Valley, 1958.

Central Nevada Historical Society –
Jacobson Collection

(Below) Loading loose cotton on
Hafen Farms for transport to gin in
Blythe, California, 1958.

Central Nevada Historical Society –
Jacobson Collection

Tim Hafen, Mesquite, Nevada, 1947.

Nye County Town History Project – Hafen Collection

California would move into the area. In 1951 Tim Hafen followed Elmer Bowman's pioneering footsteps into Pahrump.

Maxwell Kent Hafen, better known as "Tim," was born in St. George, Utah, in 1932, the oldest of four sons of Maxwell and Estelle Hafen. The senior Hafen had one of the larger farms in the Mesquite, Nevada, area. The Hafens were encouraged by Elmer Bowman to buy farmland in Pahrump because of the artesian water and cheap land. Bowman was interested in building a community in Pahrump, and he knew that the only way roads, services, and the spartan social life in the community could ever be built up was by bringing other settlers into the valley. For this reason, Bowman made Hafen and his father, who had formed a partnership, a deal that, even by modern standards, no one could refuse. The Hafens purchased 840 acres from Bowman and since the part of the old Kellogg Ranch, which they bought, was untested as far as artesian well production was concerned, Bowman agreed to put up part of the well drilling costs, with the Hafens' share to be used as down payment.

In 1951, at the age of 19, Tim Hafen and his wife became modern pioneers in the Pahrump Valley. Their first home was an old 25-foot trailer, without indoor plumbing, which they towed from North Las Vegas. Hafen recalls that between the poorly heated trailer and the makeshift shower facility, "it was a little bit cold" in the winter (M. Hafen, 1988). The Hafens lived in the trailer until 1954, at which time a more spacious 16x24-foot house was moved in from Boulder City. The house was originally built during the construction of Boulder Dam, but could not meet updated codes. Those first homes were followed by others, each bigger and better than the last.

The first year, Hafen planted 40 acres of alfalfa and the next year he planted 100 acres of cotton and more alfalfa (M. Hafen, 1988). Initially, Tim would transport his father's farming

Tim Hafen at Well No. 5 on his ranch. The artesian water flowed at between 800 and 900 gallons per minute. Lisa Hafen (left) and Miguel Arena are pictured.   Nye County Town History Project – Hafen Collection

equipment from Mesquite to Pahrump, "farm like crazy" for two or three weeks, then return the equipment to his father. The 35 miles of rock road over the Johnnie Summit meant that Hafen could count on at least one blow-out on his rayon tires per trip (M. Hafen, 1988).

Before new land could be brought under cultivation, it had to be cleared. Much of the ground that Hafen initially farmed had originally been planted in grains by Lois Kellogg, but after her death it had reverted to brush and huge tumbleweeds. These were cleared by pulling a 16-foot-long section of railroad rail across the ground. As the rail moved, it uprooted the weeds, which accumulated in a pile at the front of the rail. The pile was set on fire; if the tractor was driven at the proper speed, a continuous fire could be maintained as the rail was pulled across the ground (M. Hafen, 1988). Since Elmer Bowman had several years' experience farming, he provided young Hafen with valuable assistance and advice in adjusting to the techniques that were necessary to produce success in Pahrump. Among many other things, he showed Hafen how to properly level his rows and also the proper techniques for use of siphon irrigation as opposed to the flood irrigation, which Hafen had used in Mesquite. Ditches followed the contour of the land, Hafen recalled, and "sometimes it would look like a snake going across the land, but when you filled that ditch with water it would level and the water would be level from one end to the other." In 1963, Hafen added the 650 acres from the Frehner Ranch to his holdings. Cotton was the most important crop grown on Hafen's ranch during this period, although alfalfa and some grain were also produced (M. Hafen, 1988).

Hafen became an outstanding community leader. His leadership qualities inevitably led to politics, and he served in Nevada's General Assembly for four terms. However, he left politics at the height of his career to devote more of his time to farming.

From left: Max Hafen, Bob Ruud, and Tim Hafen celebrate the completion of a cattle chute on the Ruuds' Basin Ranch. The chute was put together in cooperation with the state of Nevada and some of the advisory council from the University of Nevada, Reno, and is used for vaccination and de-horning.
Nye County Town History Project – Hafen Collection

Ted and Marie Blosser Take to Cotton

Ted Blosser was born in Santa Maria, California, in 1916. After serving in World War II, he grew cotton on leased land in the Ivanhoe area of California, but he wanted his own farm. A friend encouraged Blosser and his father to look at land in Fish Lake Valley. They did so, spending the night in Tonopah at the Mizpah Hotel. At breakfast the next morning a stranger, overhearing Blosser and his father talking about growing cotton in Nevada, encouraged them to look at Pahrump Valley.

Blosser and his father took the stranger's advice and headed south that morning. Later that day they pulled up to Burkett's Trading Post in Pahrump. The wind was blowing hard, Blosser recalled, and when his father opened the car door and stepped out, the wind blew his hat off. A small boy standing nearby retrieved the hat and returned it to its owner. "Fellow, does the wind always blow this way?" the elder Blosser asked the helpful lad.

"No sir," the boy replied with a twinkle in his eye, "sometimes it blows the other way."

That was in 1952 and was Ted Blosser's first contact with the Pahrump Valley.

In the store, the Blossers inquired about cotton farming in Pahrump; they were advised to talk to Tim Hafen, who had been in the valley about a year. They drove to Hafen's ranch and found him in a field on a tractor. A conversation with Hafen convinced Ted to make the move.

When Blosser entered the cotton business in Pahrump, the price of cotton was 35 to 45 cents a pound, supported by the federal government. Diesel fuel was 7 cents a gallon by the truckload, and all irrigation water was pumped by diesel engines. Ted and Marie Blosser installed a 10,000-gallon diesel storage tank, purchased a 50-kilowatt generator, hooked the generator to the tank, and ran it day and night.

Like all farmers in the valley (except the very largest), Blosser did most of his own mechanical work, repairing engines and keeping equipment running. And like many cotton farmers in the valley, especially those who were forced to service debt on their farms, Ted and his wife, Marie, found it necessary to supplement their incomes through outside employment. Blosser recalled, "What it boiled down to is, I subsidized this farm to the tune of $10,000 to $12,000 a year working at the Test Site and Marie put food on the table" by teaching school in Pahrump (Blosser, 1988).

Bob and Jacque Ruud: The Pioneering Spirit

Bob and Jacque Ruud moved to the Pahrump Valley from Madera, California, in 1958. They loaded part of the furnishings from a six-room house into a 48x8-foot mobile home and headed for Pahrump. They acquired land through the Desert Land Act and purchased additional acres. From a community where telephones, television, school buses, paved roads, corner grocery stores, and one-hour equipment parts replacement were the norm, the Ruuds found themselves in an area with no electricity and no television, where the nearest "corner grocery store" was several miles away, the school buses were makeshift affairs, and if one cared to drive day and night to Lancaster, California, to replace a broken piece of farm equipment the venture took a minimum of one day. The nearest telephone was 28 miles away over dirt roads.

Jacque recalled, "I decided it would take an adventuresome pioneering spirit to live in Nevada, but we both had that, so the only way to go was forward for ourselves as well as for our family and new community" (Ruud, 1988). In 1958 Pahrump consisted of about 250 people. The Ruuds were active in community affairs and Bob filled many leadership positions, including three terms as Nye County commissioner from the Pahrump District. Bob Ruud died unexpectedly in 1982, and Jacque was appointed to serve his unexpired term.

Bob Ruud wrapping meat for the Pahrump Harvest Festival in the early 1970s. Bob was the chef for the festival for about 12 years.

Nye County Town History Project – Ruud Collection

Walt Williams: A Texan Moves to Pahrump

During the period when cotton was king in the Pahrump Valley, the largest operation was owned by Walter J. Williams. Williams had been a successful cotton grower in Pecos, Texas, in the late 1940s and 1950s, but he was seeking new opportunities. In 1957, he noticed an ad in the *Fort Worth Star-Telegram* that described a ranch consisting of 12,000 acres, 16,000 acres of leased grazing land in the hills to the east of the ranch, and a 1000-acre cotton allotment, located 60 miles west of Las Vegas. Williams knew that the cotton allotment was unusually large. One thousand acres at that time represented approximately 30 percent of the state of Nevada's allotment. Williams traveled to Nevada and inspected the ranch. It was the giant Pahrump Ranch. Here was an opportunity to grow cotton on a large scale in an area where cotton production was new but proven. In addition, Williams saw great potential for the Pahrump Valley itself. Although the area was quite isolated and lacked services, he recognized that it could experience growth because of its abundance of land and water. Williams and his partner, Frank Crews, decided to purchase the ranch.

Williams obtained the Pahrump Ranch from C. B. Dickey Associates of Arvin, California. Dickey was a cotton man who owned considerable cotton-producing and processing resources in California and his operation in Pahrump had been more of a sideline. Williams agreed to purchase the Pahrump Ranch for $400,000, at approximately $30 per acre, on a four-year lease-purchase contract, to be concluded in 1962. At the time of the purchase, there were others growing cotton in the valley: Dale and Dorothy Dorothy at the Lazy 88 Ranch; Tim Hafen; Bob and Jacque Ruud at the Basin Ranch; Ted and Marie Blosser; and the Bowman family on the Manse Ranch, among others.

Entrance to Pahrump Ranch, circa 1950.

San Bernardino County Museum – Fisk Collection

The corral on the Pahrump Ranch, about 1950. Two large grain bins are visible in the distance. Behind the corral there was a pasture.

Nye County Town History Project – Brown Collection

When Williams took over the Pahrump Ranch, he found that it had been somewhat neglected. Irrigation ditches, in particular, were in bad shape. Erosion had produced deep gullies. The fields were badly infested with weeds. Williams had to rush to plant his first crop in 1957, but by 1959 he had his full 1000 acres in cotton. Thereafter he rotated cotton and alfalfa, with a three-year rotation for each crop.

In 1959 the first and only cotton gin in Nevada was constructed in Pahrump. For many years, Jacque Ruud managed the cotton gin. It was a medium-sized facility of four 80-saw stands. The Pahrump Ranch provided the first bale of cotton to go through the new gin. No longer would farmers have to bale their cotton and have it trucked to California for processing. They could pick the cotton with traditional pickers and transport the wagons a few miles down the road. After the processing, the seed was transported by truck to Blythe, and the cotton was pressed into bales at the gin and sold to the buyer of the farmer's choice. Most farmers in the valley sold to a co-op in California.

A large number of hoers were needed because of the abundance of Johnson grass in the fields. Though herbicides were available, they were expensive, required multiple applications, and had to be applied in exactly the right way to be successful. Williams never used them. Because he spoke some Spanish and was familiar with the procedures for hiring and

Walter J. Williams at the airstrip located at the Pahrump Ranch, circa 1960. The cotton gin can be seen in the distance at the end of the airstrip.

Nye County Town History Project – Blosser Collection

working with Bracero workers from Mexico, he made many trips to Brawley, California, through the years to screen workers for himself and for other farmers in the valley.

While Williams controlled the Pahrump Ranch, there were cuts in the Bracero Program and he lost a good portion of his labor force. For a couple of years Williams was unable to obtain enough quality workers needed for his cotton fields, so he turned to a different method of weeding, one that he had seen used in Texas. Williams bought several thousand goslings from a dealer in California and had them shipped to the ranch, where he kept them in a pen for a few days to get them acclimated to the area. Then he turned the thousands of geese loose on his cotton fields, where they attacked the Johnson grass and other weeds with great enthusiasm.

Cotton, Williams explained, is a thirteen-month crop: It is more than a year-round job. By the time the last gleanings are finished around Christmas, it is time to start preparing the land for the new crop. Furthermore, most Pahrump farmers agree that the valley is not ideally suited for cotton because it is too far north and the growing season is a little short. Although the valley produced an excellent quality upland cotton, the average farmer could not get rich growing cotton in Pahrump. And a bad crop year could mean disaster; in 1965, Williams had a poor crop and lost $200,000. Expenses were enormous; the Pahrump Ranch alone used twelve 10,000-gallon loads of diesel a year. Although cotton was "king" for a time in Pahrump, the future of the valley's abundant land and water resources lay in another direction.

Williams is credited with another Nevada agricultural first. In 1967, not long after the

Exterior view of Nevada Ginning Company, Pahrump Valley, Nevada, 1960s or 1970s.

Nye County Town History Project – Hafen Collection

process was developed, he began cubing alfalfa grown on his ranch. Baling hay, he recalled, is a cumbersome, dirty, and slow process that scatters small and even large chunks of wire through the fields. With cubing, the alfalfa is cut and allowed to lie in rows until properly dried, at which time it is scooped up, sprayed with a fine mist, and pressed into cubes, which are then stored or shipped to market. Williams' cubes were trucked to Beaumont, California, to the Albers Milling Company, a subsidiary of the Carnation Company, where they were mixed with other vitamin and food products and processed into racehorse feed. One can only guess at the number of racehorse champions nurtured on Pahrump hay; in effect, a bit of the Pahrump Valley circulated in their veins.

Williams looked back with pride on his contribution to the development of Pahrump as a community. He was active, along with others, in bringing electric power and telephone service to the valley. He was instrumental in providing high-quality Mexican laborers. Williams is also credited with initiating the Fall Harvest Festival; the first was held in 1959 on the Pahrump Ranch and

Jacque Ruud stands beside a bale of cotton ginned at Nevada Ginning Company, no date, Pahrump Valley.

Nye County Town History Project – Hafen Collection

Interior of Nevada's only cotton gin, probably late 1970s. The cotton gin closed permanently in 1983.

Nye County Town History Project – Hafen Collection

featured a Mexican-style pit barbeque. For its first few years the celebration was held on the ranch; when the community center was completed, the community itself, spearheaded by Bob Ruud, took over the festival.

Doby Doc Caudill: Colorful Individualist

Robert Doby Caudill (Doby Doc) probably came to Nevada from Texas. He claimed to have been present when General Black Jack Pershing chased Pancho Villa and his men into the hills in northern Mexico. Doby Doc also contended that he had been friendly with Texas John Slaughter, the renowned sheriff of Tombstone, Arizona, in the years after that town was made famous by Wyatt Earp and the battle at the O.K. Corral. He referred to Sheriff Slaughter as "Uncle John."

Doby Doc was a colorful character, known as an individualist, and it was this trait that led him to Pahrump. During the late 1950s and the early 1960s, there was considerable fear among many Americans that the U.S. would be subject to atomic attack by the Soviet Union. The

A function held by Calcot, Ltd., a Pahrump marketing association, approximately 1962. Left to right, George Slater, manager of Pahrump's cotton gin, Walt Williams, Perry Bowman, a Calcot official (name not known), and Tim Hafen.

Nye County Town History Project – Hafen Collection

government encouraged citizens to construct fallout shelters for use in the event of an attack. Doby took this advice seriously and decided to construct a bomb shelter on property he owned on the Strip just south of the Tropicana Hotel in Las Vegas. Intent upon protecting himself from the Russians, he took his old bulldozer and started to dig a hole. The hole was getting deep when a man walked on the property and asked, "What are you doing?"

Doby Doc replied, "I'm building a bomb shelter."

The man then asked, "You got a permit?"

Doby Doc looked at him coldly and said, "I don't buy a permit from nobody" (Ford, 1988).

This problem led to Doc's "solution": He purchased Pop Buol's old place and moved to Pahrump. There he constructed a very adequate bomb shelter on his property and he did so without a permit.

While Doby Doc was in Pahrump, his old friend Benny Binion, owner of the Horseshoe Club in Las Vegas, was sent to prison for income tax problems. The Binion family brought Doby Doc in to run the club. Doby Doc had to be constantly available at the club in order to participate in the money count. Often he had to drive into Las Vegas from Pahrump every eight hours for the count. His bedroom had no windows and thus could be made completely dark; regardless of the time of day, he could come home and sleep. Someone once asked him, "Doby, why don't you hire somebody to take care of that money count?"

Doby replied, "Pretty soon he'll have as much money as me" (Ford, 1988).

The Binions purchased the old Buol place from Doby prior to his death. They used it to winter horses kept on their ranch in Montana during the summer. Harry Ford, whose front porch overlooked the Binion pasture, said it was beautiful to see over one hundred head of horses turned loose and running along the fences and to see a beautifully polished stagecoach pulled by four black horses practicing turns on the property. Many of the grapevines and fruit trees that Pop Buol planted years ago are still on the property and are still maintained, but they do not produce in the abundance they did when Buol owned them.

The Pahrump Trading Post

Originally Charles Bennett ran a store on the Pahrump Ranch. Not long after the turn of the century, Pop Buol moved to the valley, and he operated a store on his property for many years. (Buol's store was located approximately one-half mile west of the present junction of Highways 160 and 372—near the location of the A&A Market.)

Sometime prior to 1948, Pawford and Johnnie Brooks constructed a large building near the old Buol place that served a number of purposes. The building's primary function was to house a mercantile operation known as the Pahrump Trading Post, but it also served as a saloon, as living quarters for the Brooks, and as a post office. A gas pump also stood in front of the Trading Post. In 1947, the Brooks sold the operation to Vernon Ward and Guy Pinnell; Ward's parents, Tom and Fannie, joined in the partnership a short time later.

Mrs. Brooks had been the postmaster. When she decided to leave the valley, she asked "Dutch" Turner, who was then living in Las Vegas with her husband, Bill, if she would like to move to Pahrump and become the new postmaster. Dutch agreed, and Bill went to work on the Pahrump Ranch. Mrs. Brooks gave Dutch a three-hour course in how to run the post office; Dutch also helped out in the store. Dutch was associated off and on with the post office until her retirement in 1976. The Pahrump post office remained housed in the Pahrump Trading Post until the 1960s, when it was moved to an addition to the Cotton Pickin' Saloon, and eventually to its present site.

View of the Pahrump Trading Post, Pahrump, Nevada, approximately 1947. The building was constructed of railroad ties, as were a number of buildings in the valley from that era.

Nye County Town History Project – Hafen Collection

Aerial view of the Pahrump Trading Post, probably taken about 1947.

Nye County Town History Project – Hafen Collection

Education in Pahrump

Prior to 1900, and in the first decades of the twentieth century, it was necessary for Pahrump ranchers to send their children to live in other communities for their education. Parents could instruct small children in many of the basics, but as the children got older, they were sent away to school, usually to live with family. The Harsha Whites, for instance, sent their children to San Bernardino.

Ed Fleming, who had grown up in the iron ore district of northern Minnesota, obtained his first school teaching position in Pahrump in 1938. The valley had its own school district, known as the Rose School District, which was separate from the Nye County school system. Classes were held in a small building that was located on Pop Buol's property (the spot is about one-half mile west of the present junction of Highways 160 and 372). The building, which was constructed of railroad ties, had a dirt roof. "Old Pop Buol put dirt roofs on a lot of the buildings" (Ford, 1988).

When Stanley Ford moved to Pahrump in 1944, his children attended school in the same one-room schoolhouse for several months. The school went from the first to the eighth grade and there were at least fifteen students. There was no high school, so older students had to leave the valley to attend schools in other locations, such as Death Valley Junction, Shoshone, Las Vegas, and Needles, California.

A teacher at the Pahrump School in the 1930s and early 1940s was paid about $125 a month and room and board. Sometimes ranchers provided part of a bunkhouse or structure for the teacher to live in. For two years in the late 1930s Ed Fleming rented a small house that a Mrs. Miller had constructed as a "honeymoon" cottage. Ford remembered that once, in the 1940s, toward the end of the school year the school did not have enough money to pay the teacher. A bingo party was held at the old hotel on the Pahrump Ranch and women brought pies and

The Pahrump School, operated by the Rose School District, Main Street, Pahrump, 1948. The school was located just east of the entrance to the Pahrump Ranch. *Nye County Town History Project – Ford Collection*

cakes. The community raised enough money to pay the teacher's salary for the rest of the year.

From the schoolhouse on the Buol property, in the fall of 1944 classes were relocated to the red schoolhouse, which had been moved from Clay Camp in Ash Meadows to a site near the entrance to the Pahrump Ranch, on what is now Highway 372, just west of the junction with Highway 160. School was held there for eight years until a barracks building was moved in from Boulder City to the site of the present grade school on Wilson Street; three additional classrooms were constructed in the late 1950s. The red schoolhouse is presently (1990) located on property owned by Preferred Equities; there is community interest in its restoration. In about 1958 the local school district was incorporated into the Nye County School District. In 1973, a portion of the money obtained by Nye County District Attorney William P. Beko's successful property tax lawsuit against the contractors on the Nevada Test Site was used to construct (and totally fund) a new high school in Pahrump. Pahrump's steady growth led to a burgeoning school population, numbering over 1000 students in 1988. Because of the increase in population, Pahrump High School moved from the "A" to the "AA" athletic classification in southern Nevada in 1987.

Students alongside an automobile used as a school bus in Pahrump, 1945.

Nye County Town History Project – Ford Collection

Community Growth

In 1948 there were 8 ranches located in the Pahrump Valley. By 1965, there were 33 operations and a total of 7500 acres under cultivation, approximately one-third devoted to cotton. The remainder of the farm land at that time was primarily in wheat, alfalfa, and pasture. In 1968, there were approximately 10,062 acres under cultivation (the high point of production), but by 1974 that figure had fallen to 6934 acres, primarily in alfalfa but some in cotton. By 1976, six years after the sale of the giant Pahrump Ranch to Preferred Equities, cotton production had dropped to 1062 acres.

Dorothy Dorothy stated that 20 people were receiving mail through the "no postmaster" post office in 1950 and only five years later 265 people were receiving mail, with another 200 "coming and going" (Dorothy, 1955). By 1975, the population of Pahrump was estimated at 1476. Just over ten years later, the number had jumped to more than 7000, with most of the growth occurring in the 1980s.

King Cotton Deposed

Two factors spelled the end to cotton-growing in the Pahrump Valley. The first, though not necessarily the most important, was the price of cotton. In 1960, valley farmers were receiving 60 cents a pound for their cotton. By 1988, even though prices of virtually everything had tripled and quadrupled since the 1960s, the cotton price, due largely to a worldwide oversupply, was still in the 60-cent range. It was impossible for Pahrump Valley farmers to grow cotton for 60 cents a pound and survive.

The second factor was the loss of the Pahrump Ranch's cotton-growing contribution, due to the sale of the ranch to Preferred Equities. The 1000 acres of cotton that the ranch produced were essential in making Pahrump's cotton gin economically viable. Although cotton was grown on the Pahrump Ranch for a period after its sale to Preferred Equities, the eventual withdrawal of that production capacity meant that other cotton growers in the valley had to pay more to the gin in order to keep it in Pahrump. Gradually more and more farmers withdrew from growing cotton after the sale of the Pahrump Ranch; they realized that the handwriting was on the wall for the industry. The withdrawal of each farmer from cotton-growing made the gin that much more uneconomical, until all cotton production in the Pahrump Valley had ceased by the end of 1984.

Most farmers who stayed in business returned to alfalfa production. But even alfalfa was somewhat marginal. It cost a farmer in the Pahrump Valley approximately $125 an acre to irrigate alfalfa compared to $25 per acre for farmers in the Needles, Blythe, and Imperial valleys, which use Colorado River water. Although valley water costs are not that different from costs in the Central Valley Canal region and the Lancaster-Antelope Valley area in California, the distance from market is a disadvantage for Pahrump growers.

Given the heavy demands irrigation was placing on water resources, it was clear that the valley would eventually develop water shortage problems. Heavy pumping of groundwater during the decades after 1950, the heydays of the valley's agricultural period, led to unsustainable demands on the valley's water resources. In 1970, appropriations for 45,607 acre-feet per year had been certified, and permits had been granted to develop another 45,416 acre-feet per year. The total potential legal demand of more than 91,000 acre-feet per year was about four times the annual recharge rate for the Pahrump Valley aquifer. In 1970, the state engineer ordered that no more groundwater permits for irrigation be granted in the Pahrump Artesian Basin.

The Cotton Pickin' Saloon near Highway 372, Pahrump, Nevada, approximately 1970.

Nye County Town History Project – Hafen Collection

The Saddle West restaurant, early 1970s.

Nye County Town History Project – Hafen Collection

Celebrants gather at the Pahrump Harvest Festival, September 5, 1964. Looking northeast toward
Mount Sterling.

Nye County Town History Project – Ford Collection

Al and Lynn Bells baling what probably is alfalfa, on the Simkins Ranch in 1975.

Nye County Town History Project – Ruud Collection

Mike Floyd heads out of the chute during a junior rodeo in Pahrump in the mid-1970s.

Nye County Town History Project – Ruud Collection

Fall Festival Parade, Pahrump, early 1980s. The Saddle West is visible in the background.

Nye County Town History Project – Hafen Collection

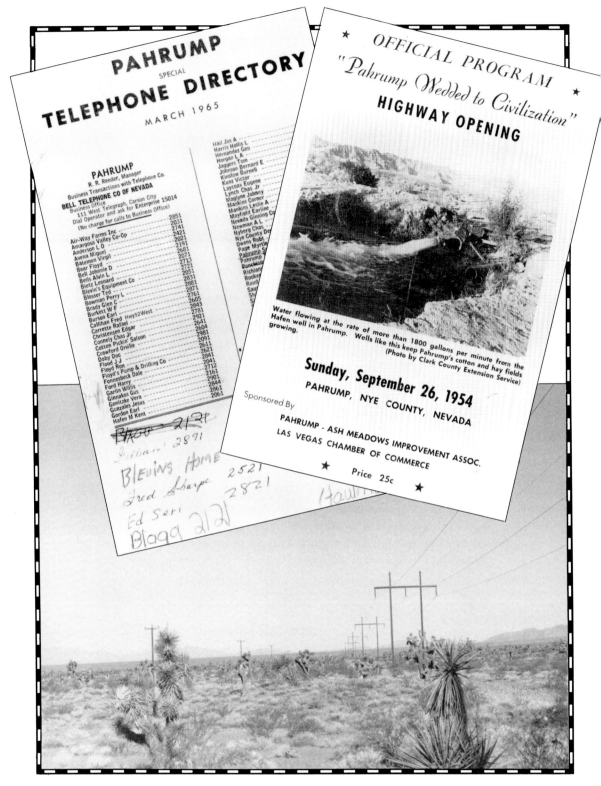

Within a ten-year period (from mid-1950s to mid-1960s), telephones, highways, and electricity gave Pahrump a new look.

Official Program for Highway Opening and Pahrump's first telephone directory courtesy of Harry Ford. Montage by Polly Christensen

CHAPTER FOUR

Three Additional Steps Toward Modernization

Cotton-growing brought people and a degree of prosperity to the Pahrump Valley. Although the population increase was not great compared to a large city, it formed the foundation upon which future growth could take place. This expansion gave impetus to the implementation of three modern services without which further growth would have been impossible. These services were paved roads, electric power, and telephones. These developments all took place within a ten-year period from the middle 1950s to the middle 1960s. They had the effect of fulfilling the promise that local writer Dorothy Dorothy had made a few years earlier:

> All this valley needs is a chance to progress. Take off the shackles, the hobbles, the stranglehold and give it the freedom through paved roads, and electricity, and watch a bonanza of the west such as you thought only a gold rush could create. This vein WILL NEVER RUN OUT! (Dorothy, n.d.).

Modern Roads and Highways

Pahrump Valley residents had dreamed of a paved road linking their community with Las Vegas for years. Lack of good roads had long stymied valley development. There were dirt roads in the valley that would take a traveler from Pahrump to the next town, but they were never well maintained; they were dusty and slow and damaged cars and tires. The most frequently used route to Las Vegas for valley residents was north over the Johnnie Summit for 26 miles to Highway 95 and then on pavement for about 68 miles into Las Vegas. This was more than a two-hour trip one way, even in the days when there was no speed limit on Highway 95. Another dirt road led south down the Pahrump Valley, through Sandy Valley to Goodsprings, and then to Jean, where one could connect with the Las Vegas-Los Angeles highway. This was an extremely long and dusty route and it might take more than 3-1/2 hours from the Pahrump Ranch. In the early 1950s a dirt road was completed over the Spring Mountains at Mountain Springs along the route of the Old Mormon Trail. It was a rough road but was used by some residents. Dirt roads also linked Pahrump with Shoshone and Tecopa, California.

The first section of paved road in the Pahrump Valley was constructed in 1953, linking the Clark County-Nye County line just north of the Manse Ranch with the north end of the valley. In 1954 Highway 160, linking Pahrump with Las Vegas over the Spring Mountains at Mountain Springs, was completed. The route was officially opened on Sunday, September 26, 1954. The official program for the celebration hailed, "Pahrump Wedded to Civilization." The road, in addition to making it easier for Pahrump residents to reach Las Vegas, was also hailed as a time-saving cutoff to communities linking Las Vegas and California.

The road connecting Pahrump with Highway 95 to the north over the Johnnie Summit was not paved until 1966. Paving of the road to Shoshone was started in 1955 and completed in 1956, and the paved road to Tecopa was completed a little later. Originally, sentiments favored paving the northern link with Highway 95 first, rather than paving the route over Mountain Springs. This may have been because many residents were familiar with that route to Las Vegas, despite the fact that it was longer than the route over Mountain Springs.

The establishment and development of the Nevada Test Site in the early 1950s led to the need for an improved road from Mercury to Pahrump. The distance from the gate at Mercury to Pahrump is only about 40 miles, at least 20 miles closer than Las Vegas is to Mercury. The 26 miles of dirt road over the Johnnie Summit effectively discouraged all but the most intrepid Test Site workers from settling in Pahrump during the early years of nuclear testing, however. Few chose to drive the 52 miles over tire-busting dirt roads every day; instead, most made the hazardous trip back and forth to Las Vegas over what became known as the Widow Maker highway because of the large number of accidents and fatalities on the road.

When the road over the Johnnie Summit to Highway 95, now Highway 160, was paved in 1966, this created a long paved loop from Las Vegas over Mountain Springs, north to Pahrump, over the Johnnie Summit to Highway 95, and then south again to Las Vegas. Former State Assemblyman Robert A. Revert, a resident of Beatty, was instrumental in obtaining authorization for paving the route, and he looked back with pride on his role in helping to link Pahrump with Las Vegas.

The paving of both the Johnnie and Mountain Springs roads led to a steady influx of Test Site workers and others who moved to Pahrump. Some moved there because they liked open spaces, fresh air, and freedom from the hustle and bustle of the increasingly large city of Las Vegas. Since Pahrump was located in Nye County, which had no building codes or building restrictions, many were attracted to Pahrump because they were free to construct the type of home they wanted or could afford. In Pahrump, a worker was free to set up a small mobile home, drill his well, install a septic tank, and have a horse corral, all free from the harassment of building inspectors and city bureaucrats. Often, a family would move to Pahrump and live in humble circumstances for a time. But by saving their money and working hard they could gradually improve their circumstances until finally they had a nice home of their own on their own acreage, something of which both they and the community could be proud. In contrast, someone who had located in Las Vegas might have accumulated a large stack of rent receipts and little else. This sense of freedom is still enjoyed by Pahrump residents.

Electric Power Comes to the Pahrump Valley

In the days before electric power arrived on powerlines, Pahrump Valley residents used generators for household needs. This was an awkward arrangement because the generators were expensive, needed to be serviced regularly, and were subject to mechanical breakdowns.

In addition, it was inconvenient to start and stop the engines in the evening or when power was needed, unless one ran the generator all day, in which case the expense was even greater. In most cases the generators were small and care had to be exercised concerning the load that was put on the supply at any one time. The lack of a public electric power system in the Pahrump Valley was probably the second biggest impediment to growth and development, after the lack of good roads.

When Harry Ford got married in 1958, he and his bride had a small propane-fired generator that was adequate for the house if one didn't run many things at a time. In the summer, Ford remembered, "it would run the electric washing machine and a swamp cooler, but not both at the same time" (Ford, 1988).

Bringing power to the Pahrump Valley was not easy; it took a struggle. Valley farmers began talking about the problems in the early 1950s. They attended meetings and formed a small cooperative utility company known as the Pahrump Valley Utility Company. In the middle and late 1950s, leaders held meetings with the Nevada Power Company in Las Vegas, attempting to induce the large utility to build lines into Pahrump. These efforts were futile. Pahrump, as far as the utility was concerned, was unproven and did not represent a potential profit.

Meanwhile, ranchers in the Amargosa Valley were working along the same lines to bring power to their valley. H. H. (Hank) Records had moved to the Amargosa Valley in 1953; in 1957 he took over the old Tonopah and Tidewater Ranch. He and his brother Robert, along with Ed Mankinen, Ralph Dalton, and Gene Eastabrooks, had formed the Amargosa Valley Electric Cooperative. Like their neighbors in the Pahrump Valley, they had attempted to interest the Nevada Power Company in extending service and they, too, had been rebuffed.

Hank Records had lined up engineers in Albuquerque, New Mexico, to conduct a feasibility study on bringing power into the Amargosa and Pahrump valleys and had touched a number of political bases as well. He knew an official at the Nevada Test Site and suggested that the Test Site could use a backup power source. At that time, the Nevada Power Company supplied power to the Nevada Test Site, but outages sometimes occurred. If an alternative power source were available, Test Site activities would not be subject to disruption when the Nevada Power Company source was broken, Records argued. Test Site officials agreed, and they worked with the Amargosa Valley Electric Co-Op.

The support of the Atomic Energy Commission provided the extra clout needed for the residents of the two valleys. The Pahrump and Amargosa valley cooperatives merged in March 1963, and three days later the REA approved a loan for $3.9 million. The new cooperative constructed the 120-mile transmission line and 300 miles of distribution lines that brought power to Pahrump, Amargosa Valley, and Beatty from Hoover Dam.

Telephone Service Reaches the Valley

For years the nearest phone for Pahrump Valley residents was located in Shoshone, California. Although area residents had approached Nevada Bell many times to request the installation of telephone service, the answer only mimicked Nevada Power's response regarding electricity. In 1964, the Amargosa Valley Power Cooperative (Valley Electric Association) obtained a loan commitment from the REA to construct a telephone system in Pahrump. Threat of the cooperative constructing and operating its own phone system provided an incentive for Nevada Bell to obtain Public Service Commission approval and construct a telephone system in Pahrump in 1964. The valley's phone system has since been upgraded several times and the system in operation in 1989 was the equivalent of any in the United States.

By 1970, as these pages from the *Nevada West and Pahrump Valley Times* indicate, subdivision in the Pahrump Valley was well under way.

Courtesy Harry Ford. Montage by Polly Christensen

CHAPTER FIVE

Subdivision Begins in Pahrump

With plenty of land and water, clean air, and a pollution-free environment, as well as good paved roads, reasonably priced electric power, and telephone service, the stage finally was set for Pahrump to fulfill its destiny and begin to become a city. A final necessary step was for the large land holdings to be divided into smaller parcels that buyers could purchase to construct homes on.

The first serious subdivision effort in Pahrump Valley began in about 1959 or 1960 on the valley's west side. A group of Los Angeles lawyers, including Bud Corbin, purchased large parcels on the west side of the valley, subdivided the land on paper, and filed maps with Nye County. These lots were sold for $495 an acre with $50 down and $50 a month. They were sold primarily through *Stars and Stripes*, a magazine for servicemen. These subdivisions were called Charleston Park Ranchos and Cal-Vegas Ranchos, Units 1-6, and they sold by the hundreds. In addition, Jim Lawrence subdivided about 160 acres on Leslie Street, and Stanley Ford subdivided 160 acres that he had obtained through trades for drilling wells. Ford sold eight lots for $100 down, $25 a month, and 5 percent interest. Ford's was some of the first subdivided land in the valley on which people moved shortly after their purchase. Subdivision during this period, until about 1970, was confined to the west side of the valley because the good farmland was on the east side.

The first person to subdivide on the east side of the valley was Jim Raycraft, in the area of West, East, Center, and Wilson streets. He subdivided 80 acres into 1-acre lots, minus the area used for the road. In 1961, he charged $250 for these lots, at the same time that a person could buy 40 acres for $60 an acre.

In 1970 Preferred Equities purchased the 10,000 acres remaining in the Pahrump Ranch from Walt Williams and his partner. Preferred Equities was a land development company owned by Leonard Rosen and his family. Leonard and Jack Rosen were remarkable figures in the annals of American business. They used television in innovative ways for sales promotion, developed communities in Florida and elsewhere, and created sales techniques that remain basic in the marketing of land. Leonard Rosen had always wanted to build an ideal community, one that was both aesthetically pleasing and designed to meet the needs of its residents as effectively as possible.

In 1950 Leonard Rosen and his wife took a trip to the west coast and stopped off in Las Vegas. Rosen was immediately smitten by the desert, its wide open spaces, and stark, natural beauty. They stayed at the Desert Inn and purchased a block of land. Although Rosen intended to become involved in business in Las Vegas at that time, his wife's unexpected pregnancy prevented such a move. Yet the Rosens were sufficiently enchanted by the desert to name the baby girl Sandy in honor of the desert sands of Las Vegas. As Linda Rosen Sterling, another Rosen daughter, said, quoting her father, "'Instead of sand, we got Sandy'" (Sterling and Venze, 1988). Rosen never forgot Las Vegas and in the back of his mind seemed always to have planned to return.

Rosen had recognized that the sunbelt of the United States had great potential for population growth and that Las Vegas was a city with an enormously bright future. He knew that most of southern Nevada was owned by the federal government and that any development was constrained by the availability of water. He recognized that land in the Las Vegas Valley was far too expensive for the kind of development he had accomplished in Florida and which he had in mind for Nevada. He knew that Pahrump Valley had both the water and land.

Thus, Preferred Equities purchased the Pahrump Ranch in 1970 for $3.5 million on a seven-year contract. The corporation began to develop the big Pahrump Ranch almost immediately. Large numbers of lots were laid out, streets were constructed, and an active sales program undertaken under the direction of Jack Soules. Lots were sold over the next fifteen years, with the focus of sales activity in Las Vegas.

Preferred Equities immediately became the leading force in the valley for the development of Pahrump into a modern community. Through the years the company acquired additional large properties in the valley, including several large acreages at the north end. Gradually the Pahrump Ranch was withdrawn from agricultural production and so were additional farm properties that the company purchased.

A shift of the Pahrump Ranch from farming to land sales served as a catalyst, and other land owners in the valley soon followed suit. Farmers like Ted Blosser and Tim Hafen subdivided parts of their properties not then under cultivation, and though they continued farming after subdividing, they recognized that the future of the valley was not in farming, but in land development.

Pahrump's Modern Indians and Mexican Americans

Not many Native Americans remain in the Pahrump Valley; the population is very small in comparison to former times. In 1988, there were 33 Native Americans living in the Pahrump Valley and outlying areas, consisting of 14 households. Many are Southern Paiute; most of the remainder are Shoshone. Descendants of Chief Tecopa and Whispering Ben still reside in the valley. Although they are integrated into white society in many ways, individuals do make an effort to preserve aspects of their Indian identity and vestiges of their earlier culture.

There were no Mexican Americans in substantial numbers living in the Pahrump Valley prior to the cotton boom beginning about 1950. After Walt Williams' purchase of the Pahrump Ranch in 1957, Mexican Americans from Texas and Mexico entered the valley in relatively large numbers as laborers in the cotton fields. Often they brought their families with them or sent for them not long after arriving. Over the years, these residents have become thoroughly integrated into the Pahrump community and are highly respected by their neighbors for their hard work and high moral standards. As farming in the Pahrump community has ebbed, Mexican-American families have shifted to other occupations, although some remain in farming.

The Future of the Valley

Pahrump's future will be as a small city rather than an agricultural community. This urban community will provide the goods and services any small sunbelt city offers. Pahrump will be particularly attractive for retirees and for those who prefer a quiet lifestyle, with plenty of empty space, a salubrious climate, and clean air and water. Moreover, its land prices are virtually unbeatable when compared with anything similar in the United States. It will also be attractive to those who are earning a living in the increasingly congested Las Vegas Valley and who prefer to commute to a home in the Pahrump Valley, using the driving time to listen to music, enjoy the scenery, or organize their thoughts.

No one can predict the long-range destiny of the Pahrump Valley (or any community). We have no way of knowing what generations 250 or 500 years from now will be like, what technology they will possess, what their attitudes toward life and the land will be. Yet the history of a community, the study of its past, should provide some idea about where it is heading in the historical short term, say, the next 25 or 50 years. In this regard, there can be little doubt. Since the white man first took possession of the valley from the Indians, though there was plenty of good farmland and water, the valley was never very successful economically. Its isolation and distance to markets always retarded any full development. Pahrump had a brief period of agricultural prosperity in the 1950s and 1960s with cotton, and to a lesser extent with alfalfa, but it was clear even then to the careful observer what Pahrump "should be." Given the geography of the American West and the relative scarcity of water and privately owned land, the Pahrump Valley's destiny is clear: It is to be a small city. It is not a city yet, but it almost inevitably will become one.

An old wagon wheel symbolizes the Pahrump Valley's pioneer past.

San Bernardino County Museum – Fisk Collection

References

Blosser, Theodore L. *An Interview with Theodore L. Blosser.* Nye County Town History Project, Tonopah, NV. 1988.

Bowman, Perry. *An Interview with Perry Bowman.* Nye County Town History Project, Tonopah, NV. 1988.

Brooks, Thomas W. *By Buckboard to Beatty: The California-Nevada Desert in 1886.* Edited, with introduction and notes by Anthony Lehman. Los Angeles: Dawson's Book Shop. 1970.

Carlson, Helen. *Nevada Place Names: A Geographical Dictionary.* Reno: University of Nevada Press. 1974.

Dorothy, Dorothy. "And a Dream of Many Years Came True." *Nevada Highways and Parks.* January-April 1955.

———. "Pumpings from Pahrump." Copies of selected newspaper columns by author. Courtesy Tim Hafen. Pahrump, NV. n.d.

Ford, Harry "Button." *An Interview with Harry "Button" Ford.* Nye County Town History Project, Tonopah, NV. 1988.

Hafen, M. Kent "Tim." *An Interview with M. Kent "Tim" Hafen.* Nye County Town History Project, Tonopah, NV. 1988.

Hughes, Leon. *An Interview with Leon Hughes.* Nye County Town History Project, Tonopah, NV. 1988.

"Indian Powwow: Remnants of the Paiute Tribe Meet at Pahrump." *Las Vegas Age*. September 30, 1905.

Kelly, Isabel T., and Catherine S. Fowler. "Southern Paiute" in *Great Basin*, Warren L. D'Azevedo, ed. Vol. 11 of *Handbook of North American Indians*, pp. 368-397. Washington, DC: Smithsonian Institution. 1986.

Lingenfelter, Richard E. *Death Valley and the Amargosa: A Land of Illusion*. Berkeley: University of California Press. 1986.

Lowe, Deke. *An Interview with Deke Lowe*. Nye County Town History Project, Tonopah, NV. 1988.

Mottaz, Stan. "County Evolution in Nevada." *Nevada Historical Society Quarterly*, vol. 21, no. 1, pp. 25-49. Spring 1978.

Rafferty, Kevin, and Lynda Blair. *Billy Goat Peak: An Investigation and Reinterpretation of Virgin Anasazi and Paiute Prehistory and Ethnohistory*. DAS Report 2-5-9. Las Vegas: University of Nevada, Environmental Research Center. March 1984.

While this photograph was in storage, about half of it was eaten by mice! The building in the background, called the Old Stagecoach Hotel, was located on the Pahrump Ranch. Leon Hughes believes it was used when the Pahrump Ranch was a stage stop. The building featured a screened porch, kitchen, dining room, and a hallway with four rooms on one side and three on the other. The Hughes brothers slept on the porch during the summer months in beds that were propped up on blocks to make them level. The building was said to have burned down in 1944. From left: Mabel Ishmael, Red Hughes, Beryl Hughes, and Leon Hughes; about 1938.

Nye County Town History Project – Hughes Collection

Reeder, Ray M. The Mormon Trail: A History of the Salt Lake to Los Angeles Route to 1869. Unpublished Ph.D. dissertation. Brigham Young University, Provo, UT. May 1966.

Ruud, Jacque. *An Interview with Jacque Ruud*. Nye County Town History Project, Tonopah, NV. 1988.

Sterling, Linda Rosen, and Paul Venze. *An Interview with Linda Rosen Sterling and Paul Venze*. Nye County Town History Project, Tonopah, NV. 1988.

Townley, Carrie Miller. "Helen J. Stewart: First Lady of Las Vegas. Part 2." *Nevada Historical Society Quarterly*, vol. 17, no. 1, pp. 2-27. Spring 1974.

Venstrom, Cruz. *Economic Study of Southern Nevada: Preliminary Report, 1932*. Reno: University of Nevada, Agricultural Experiment Station. 1932.

Warren, Elizabeth von Till. "Armijo's Trace Revisited: A New Interpretation of the Impact of the Antonio Armijo Route of 1829-1830 on the Development of the Old Spanish Trail." Unpublished M.A. thesis. University of Nevada, Las Vegas. May 1974.

Wiley, Roland. *An Interview with Roland Wiley*. Nye County Town History Project, Tonopah, NV. 1988.

Williams, Walter J. *An Interview with Walter J. Williams*. Nye County Town History Project, Tonopah, NV. 1988.

About the Author

Robert D. McCracken, a descendant of three generations of hardrock miners, was born in the high country of Colorado, where he lived until he was eight. His love for Nevada and its people began in the 1950s when he and his brother helped his father operate mines at several sites in Nye County, including Reveille Valley and Silver Bow. During his college years, McCracken worked in Nye County on construction jobs. He earned his Ph.D. in cultural anthropology at the University of Colorado and has taught at Colorado Women's College, California State University at Long Beach, and UCLA. He is the author of numerous scientific reports and articles and was cited in *Time* for his work on human evolution. In 1981 he returned to Tonopah, where his father had retired. He began the Nye County Town History Project in 1987.

Books from Nye County Press

by Robert D. McCracken

A History of Amargosa Valley, Nevada (cloth)
 ISBN: 1-878138-56-1

The Modern Pioneers of the Amargosa Valley (paper)
 ISBN: 1-878138-58-8

A History of Beatty, Nevada (cloth)
 ISBN: 1-878138-54-5

Beatty: Frontier Oasis (paper)
 ISBN: 1-878138-55-3

A History of Pahrump, Nevada (cloth)
 ISBN: 1-878138-51-0

Pahrump: A Valley Waiting to Become a City (paper)
 ISBN: 1-878138-53-7

A History of Tonopah, Nevada (cloth)
 ISBN: 1-878138-52-9

*Tonopah: The Greatest, the Richest, and the Best
 Mining Town in the World* (paper)
 ISBN: 1-878138-50-2

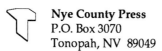 **Nye County Press**
P.O. Box 3070
Tonopah, NV 89049